MW01245004

Web-Based Infrastructures:
A 4D Framework

ISBN 0-13-032989-4

HARRIS KERN'S ENTERPRISE COMPUTING INSTITUTE

▼ Software Development: Building Reliable Systems
  Marc Hamilton

▼ High Availability: Design, Techniques, and Processes
  Michael Hawkins, Floyd Piedad

▼ Data Warehousing: Architecture and Implementation
  Mark Humphries, Michael W. Hawkins, Michelle C. Dy

▼ IT Organization: Building a Worldclass Infrastructure
  Harris Kern, Stuart D. Galup, Guy Nemiro

▼ Building Professional Services: The Sirens' Song
  Thomas E. Lah, Steve O'Connor, Mitchel Peterson

▼ IT Automation: The Quest for Lights Out
  Howie Lyke with Debra Cottone

▼ Managing IT as an Investment: Partnering for Success
  Ken Moskowitz, Harris Kern

▼ Web-Based Infrastructures: A 4D Framework
  Sanmay Mukhopadhyay, Cooper Smith with Mayra Muniz

▼ IT Systems Management
  Rich Schiesser

▼ Technology Strategies
  Cooper Smith

▼ IT Services: Costs, Metrics, Benchmarking, and Marketing
  Anthony F. Tardugno, Thomas R. DiPasquale, Robert E. Matthews

▼ IT Problem Management
  Gary Walker

HARRIS KERN'S ENTERPRISE COMPUTING INSTITUTE

Web-Based Infrastructures: A 4D Framework

**Sanmay Mukhopadhyay
Cooper Smith
with Mayra Muniz**

Prentice Hall PTR, Upper Saddle River, NJ 07458
www.phptr.com

Library of Congress Cataloging-in-Publication Data

Mukhopadhyay, Sanmay.

   Web-based infrastructures : a 4D framework / Sanmay Mukhopadhyay, Cooper Smith,
with Mayra Muniz.
      p.cm. -- (Harris Kern's Enterprise computing institute)
   ISBN 0-13-032989-4
   1. Web sites. 2. Electronic commerce. I. Smith, Cooper. II. Muniz, Mayra. III. Title.
   IV. Series.

TK5105.888.M84 2002
025.04--dc21   2002075292

Editorial/Production Supervision: *Donna Cullen-Dolce*
Executive Editor: *Greg Doench*
Editorial Assistant: *Brandt Kenna*
Marketing Manager: *Debby van Dijk*
Manufacturing Manager: *Alexis R. Heydt*
Cover Design Direction: *Jerry Votta*
Cover Design: *Talar Boorujy*
Series Design: *Gail Cocker-Bogusz*

 © 2003 Pearson Education, Inc.
Publishing as Prentice-Hall PTR
Upper Saddle River, NJ 07458

Prentice Hall books are widely used by corporations and government agencies for training,
marketing, and resale.

For information regarding corporate and government bulk discounts please contact:
Corporate and Government Sales (800) 382-3419 or corpsales@pearsontechgroup.com.
Or write: Prentice Hall PTR, Corporate Sales Dept., One Lake Street, Upper Saddle River, NJ 07458.

Printed in the United States of America

10 9 8 7 6 5 4 3 2 1

ISBN 0-13-032989-4

Pearson Education LTD.
Pearson Education Australia PTY, Limited
Pearson Education Singapore, Pte. Ltd.
Pearson Education North Asia Ltd.
Pearson Education Canada, Ltd.
Pearson Educación de Mexico, S.A. de C.V.
Pearson Education—Japan
Pearson Education Malaysia, Pte. Ltd.

Contents

Chapter 2

Why the 4D Framework?   37

Part 2

Into the Matrix   57

Chapter 3

The First Dimension: E-Drivers   63

Chapter 4

The Second Dimension: Phased Implementation   69

Chapter 6

Value Chain Program and Value Chain Linking   105

Chapter 9

Implementing the E-Change Management Process   179

Chapter 10

Case Study: Fictitious ABC Company

Part 5
Appendices   237

Appendix A

Assessment   239

Appendix B

E-Business Project Management   243

Preface

Technology and business have been working hand in hand, literally, for centuries. The last 50 years have ushered in first the Electronic Age and now the Digital Age. Never has the potential marriage of technology and business meant so much to so many. In just the last 10 years alone, the leap from the Digital Age to the Internet Age promised to go beyond the potential of landing on the moon. However, as high as the Internet rocket rose, it crashed. Why? Were expectations set too high for too long? Were the American business markets too greedy, too avaricious, too anxious to strike it rich?

Perhaps. Greed is nothing new, and the Internet rage of the 1990s is not much different than any other Gold Rush. A few actually do get rich, many more fail, but almost everyone tries their hand one way or another to grab the brass ring. Although the Gold Rush of 1849 created thousands or even hundreds of millionaires, it also helped create the city of San Francisco and eventually the San Francisco Bay area. Once the hype and the hoopla settled down, a small port town nestled in a raw windy bay found itself engulfed in a population doing what most populations do: eat, sleep, drink, work, and, hopefully, earn a living—first with their hands and now 150 years later with their minds. Yet the results of those 150 years, no matter how they started, are undeniable. Once miners seeking gold flocked to this little town; 150 years later their descendants are the doctors, lawyers, engineers, and academics who now breathe life into Silicon Valley.

No doubt, by the time the next century rolls around the Internet Gold Rush will have had as much historical significance as San Francisco's, perhaps even more, for in reality it is still going on. The Internet, although without the hype, without the fanfare, is still going strong and growing every day. The ubiquitousness of the "Net" is slowly taking route, albeit late for some, but just in time for the real revolution that is taking place throughout the world: the quiet, unassuming revolution that is here to stay, the effects of which businessman, technologists, and consumers, can only guess at over the next few decades.

Hopefully, by now we have learned that the Internet in and of itself is not the magic elixir that makes all of a business's ills disappear. It will not make us all instant millionaires. But we are starting to look analytically at what it can and does do. Business is all about communication and that is where the real evolution lies. Business and businesspeople now realize they cannot view the Internet as a separate entity to be exploited in and of itself. It, too, is a tool, like any other. Like the networks it runs on, like the computers that access it, it must be incorporated into any business the same way. The Internet is a means to an end, not the end, itself.

With that in mind, this book hopes to shed some light on our views of what kind of strategies business should and do employ to bring about some of the old-fashioned business objects of competitive advantage, productivity gain, and, yes, old-fashioned profit. The 4D Framework will probably not be the only business strategy on how to use the Internet to its maximum effectiveness in the next few years, nor will it be the last. But we do hope it will be the most useful.

Acknowledgments

From Sanmay Mukhopadhyay—So many people have helped shape my thoughts and outlook, which have resulted in this book. My dad, Santosh, and mom, Maya, who always taught me to think big and holistically. My wife, Simonti, who encouraged me to continue working on this demanding project. My kids, Sharanya and Sharthak, who sacrificed their playtime on and off. Thanks to Mayra for her hard work in creating the art and making innumerable changes to the original draft. To Ross Drogoszewski, Tom Swysgood, and Eric Lemons of Sun Microsystems, Inc., for their trust in my methodology—especially at a time when only technology was thought to be the silver bullet for corporate productivity and profitability. Thanks to all who helped me indirectly or directly in the development of the 4D process.

From Cooper Smith—For Cooper, Jr., who'll be far better at this than me, and Lancaster Stewart…just because.

From Mayra L. Muniz—In honor of my husband, who has always been supportive of my ambitions, to my mother and kids, who've been my pillars of strength during stressful times, and to my best friends (my Big Sis's) for just being there.

Part 1

What Is an E-Business?

▶ The New Playing Field

The last few years have been quite tumultuous when it comes to the Internet and real-world business applications. Our theory is that this is partly because of the mistake most financiers, investors, corporate management, etc., have made in assuming that the Internet was not a means to an end but an end in and of itself. In other words, the late 1990s had a lot of venture capital poured into ideas on how make the Internet fit into tried and true business models of the 20th century. Obviously, very few of these models actually worked. Now we are in the 21st century, and as the Internet itself matures, it is a good a time to begin devising more up-to-date business models that reflect not only what the Internet can do, but *should* do. We don't have to abandon all the business principles and concepts that have taken years to devise and perfect all at once, however. We merely have to choose new paradigms to apply them. Let's start with the simple concept of using the advantages of the Internet to simply supplement an already thriving concern as follows:

> The Internet affects operational effectiveness and strategic positioning in very different ways. It makes it harder for companies to sustain operational advantages, but it opens new opportunities for achieving and strengthening a distinctive strategic positioning.[1]

In short, this quote describes in economic terms what has happened to many companies' Internet business strategies in the past couple of years, but its meaning is not immediately intuitive unless one knows just what "operational effectiveness" and "strategic positioning" mean. This book will hopefully clarify these terms for technologists, economists, and simple businesspeople, along with many other "principles" that the New Economy will both manifest and sustain.

The worlds of technology and business have been coming together to shape our lives since the dawn of the Industrial Revolution. Over the past 50 years, the role of digital technology in shaping business has grown exponentially. In the past 20 years, we have seen digital technology enter, change, and improve every facet of our lives.

Today we are standing on the verge of the next revolution, the Digital Revolution! Like it or not, the Internet has entered both our business and our personal lives and it is here to stay. We have all heard about its

---

1.   Porter, Michael E., "Strategy and the Internet," *Harvard Business Review*, April 16, 2001.

limitless potential, but many of us are still somewhat perplexed as to how to make use of this potential. In our personal lives, the amount of information we have at our disposal is astounding! In our business lives, how do we take all that information and turn it into an honest dollar? The late 1990s turned everything from groceries to funerals into "dot-coms." Fortunes were made overnight and lost just as quickly. With the flurry of technological productivity during the period, this rapid boom-and-bust cycle was baffling to some, predictable to others. Apparently, the business models have yet to catch up with the technology models, but the revolution is well under way and universally unstoppable.

With this in mind, it is becoming ever more imperative that today's business leaders take a more educated and proactive approach to managing, leveraging, and integrating digital technology into traditional business and, in some cases, cutting-edge technology businesses. Although terms like "e-commerce" have recently fallen out of favor with Wall Street, this is primarily due to a skewed market created by unrealistic expectations and the wild speculation of the "Internet craze" of the late 1990s. The technology itself is robust, viable, and inescapable. However, new technology requires new business rules; these rules can still be based on the ongoing business principles that have been used for millennia.

The intertwining of technology and business is nothing new. It has been and will be studied by the brightest minds in both disciplines. But whether you are a technologist, economist, or simple businessperson, there is no denying that the introduction of the Internet, for better or worse, has and will continue to change the way many of us do business. But, finding the right formula for many companies has been like finding the Holy Grail. Why?

In this book, we will develop a framework that combines both qualitative business theories and ideas and quantitative practical methods for planning and creating businesses designed specifically for competing successfully on, with, and through the Internet. This framework, which we call the Four-Dimensional Framework of E-Business Development (4D Framework for short) will simplify the process of developing any e-business, encompassing everyone from the high-level business strategist down to the hands-on software developer.

The 4D Framework comprises a 4 x 4 matrix of ideas and practices that guides both the business strategist and project implementer in how to steer a course for implementing any Internet-based strategy, whether that strategy is to establish an all-encompassing Internet business like Yahoo! or Amazon.com or just to add a Web site to an established "brick-and-mortar" business.

The 4D Framework matrix envisions designing, creating, and implementing an Internet-based enterprise as a traditional IT initiative. Indeed, by the very definition of the Internet, any initiative that incorporates the Internet is a marriage of technology and business and should be approached as such. In this way, we can borrow freely from established models of project management, software development, and technical forecasting as well as add our own unique flavor to incorporate the unique advantages and disadvantages only the Internet has to offer.

Let's start with a very high-level overview of the 4D Framework. First, let's take a close look at the fundamental building blocks/drivers we will be dealing with:

- Business drivers
- People drivers
- Process drivers
- Technology drivers

Second, the required disciplines for identifying, coordinating, and implementing specific strategies include:

- E-project management disciplines, which address projects in the e-world particularly
- Value chain methodology, including value chain analysis and redesign

Finally, the following elements of "e-project implementation" will be considered:

- High-velocity management process
- Change management

Each of these subjects can be and has been studied, explored, and extrapolated on as its own separate discipline within project management, quality management system analysis, business analysis techniques, etc. However, we will try to focus on how to combine these techniques to both define and deliver viable Internet-based applications and businesses.

Before we continue, there is one thing that is vitally important to understand. An e-business is still a business and follows the same definitions and requirements as any business. We will assume that it should make a profit and that it must sustain itself within a competitive marketplace like any other business. It is not the definition of an "e-business" that is fundamentally different from an Old Economy, traditional business, but its marketplace, the "e-marketplace," which makes all the difference in the world.

Drivers of the E-World

▶ Introduction

If you are reading this book, chances are that you are well aware of the influence the Internet has had on the world so far. That impact, however, is very different if we look at the Internet from either a personal point of view or from a business perspective. The Internet has proven infinitely bountiful as a tool for personal gratification but has been much more elusive in meeting the black and white goals of a business initiative. There are many other books and documents that go into why this is so. The purpose of this book, more or less, is to present at least, our point of view as to what to do about this business perspective problem.

The "cyberworld" is much more complex than the old-fashioned "brick-and-mortar." The simple mantra of "Location! Location! Location!" has a whole new meaning when it comes cyberspace. But if the Internet is to be used for business purposes, how do apply the old rule to the new media? We can follow Michael E. Porter's advice:

> If average profitability is under pressure in many industries influenced by the Internet, it becomes important for individual

companies to set themselves apart from the pack—to be more profitable than the average performer.[1]

This is good advice, but it is easier said than done. We do not need to go into how much has already been said about the business potential of the Internet—too much has probably been said already. Our job is to define methodologies to tap into and exploit that potential to its fullest. A major mistake that has been made by the business community is seeing the Internet as a "cost-cutting" strategy to provide the same goods and services an organization already supplies. In other words, the business mantra of the past has been, "Yes, we sell widgets, but now we can sell widgets online at a fraction of the cost of maintaining a brick-and-mortar operation." This approach has led many organizations to concentrate solely on "operational effectiveness" as a means of adding value to their business.

Simply put, if we make widgets at the same cost, sell them at the same price, but reduce the cost of selling them, we increase our profit! In isolation, this seems like a good idea, but we must remember economies work under market conditions, usually with some level of competition. Real economic value relies on maintaining a competitive advantage. If everybody else who sells widgets decides to sell widgets online for the same exact reason, where is the competitive advantage?

This is why the Four-Dimensional (4D) Framework goes further than just creating a Web site and calling it an "e-business." The Internet is only an enabler for a more well-planned approach to gaining a more powerful and strategic position within a competitive market, regardless of what that market might be. To do so, we need to focus on just what that strategic position should be. There is no one-stop solution here since every organization and every business is different, with its own sets of goals, motives, and strategies. But with a fundamental understanding of how one's own business works, using our framework should illuminate the most likely paths to identifying and implementing sound Internet strategies for any form of business.

We begin by stepping away from technology for the moment and concentrating on some basic principles. This way, we can clarify and understand our strategic goals. Let's isolate these business principles and use them to define an entirely different set of business rules that

---

1. Porter, Michael E., *Competitive Advantage: Creating and Sustaining Superior Performance* (New York: Free Press, 1998).

Chapter **1** I Drivers of the E-World

provide for a more practical and successful framework for using "e-technology" to establish "e-businesses." We base these principles on what we call fundamental *drivers*:

- Business drivers
- People drivers
- Process drivers
- Technology drivers

A "driver" can be thought of as the natural cause and effect of any natural transaction. Business, after all, is the exchange of goods between two or more parties, hopefully for the benefit of both. A transaction is an isolated exchange of a good, a service performed, or a payment made. A driver is the motivation and result combined for any given transaction.

Let's look at a very simple example. Say a group of prehistoric cavepeople are hungry. If they could kill a woolly mammoth, they could all eat the meat, wear the fur, use the bones for tools, and the entire group would be better off. Since no single caveperson can kill a woolly mammoth on his or her own, they have to rely on each other, to benefit both as a group and as individuals. It serves their best interests to work together. This is a simple *business driver*.

Now that it has been decided that our cavepeople will work together, we need some structure to make sure they can work together effectively. We need a leader, of course, someone to make decisions for the group under stress or at other times of need. And there is likely to be some level of specialization. Some cavepeople may be good at running, so they should be the ones to distract the mammoth while those who are good with spears sneak up on it. Others may be good at skinning and cleaning the carcass or lighting the fires to cook it. Mind you, each member of the group may be able to do all of these things, but invariably, some will be better at some things than at others. How people work separately and how they work together, their skills and knowledge, define the *people drivers*.

Jobs, whether performed separately or in a group, are generally performed in a specific way. Sometimes, jobs can be done simultaneously, while others cannot be done until others are complete. For example, fires can be lit to cook a mammoth before it is actually killed, but of course, it can't be cooked until the mammoth is killed. Therefore, the cooks must rely on the hunters to do their job before they can do the cooking. However, the fire starters need only know *how* to start their fires. When they start them is important, but not essential for them to do their jobs. The process of rubbing sticks or striking flint is independent and included in the overall process of killing and cooking a woolly mammoth. This defines the *process drivers*.

Finally, using spears to kill the mammoth may be less effective than using poison arrows. However, making spears is considerably easier than collecting and processing effective poisons to put on the tips of arrows. There is an economic tradeoff between using one technology and using another. After all, a hunter is only going to be as good as the tools he or she uses to do the job. The tradeoff between stone spears and poison arrows is an example of a *technology driver*.

The way these drivers are listed above exemplifies their order of importance. Without the need for food and warmth, there is no need to kill a mammoth in the first place. If our cavepeople were on a South Sea island where fish and fruit were plentiful and it was always warm, there would be no business driver to kill a woolly mammoth (plus the fact that on such an island, there would be no woolly mammoths to kill). Secondly, without people willing and able to do the job, there would be no threats to any woolly mammoth. Thirdly, even if there are people who decide to take on the job of hunting the mammoth, unless they know and coordinate what they are doing, their chances of success are pretty slim. The "enterprise" should then and only then begin to look at the tools available to get the job accomplished.

One of the major flaws of the Internet boom of the late 1990s was the all-out effort to fit the business models to the technology instead of the technology to the business models. Again, using our previous example, let's say one of our cavepeople (a man) stumbles across a loaded elephant gun while hunting (we'll ignore the obvious anachronism for now). He pulls the trigger, creates a frightening explosion, and almost blows his foot off. Well, this leaves quite an impression and he decides this thing is quite an attention-getter. He brings it back to e-design and fires it off in celebration of another successful woolly mammoth hunt! This makes him very popular among his fellow cavepeople. Now we can say to ourselves, "Use the gun to go shoot a woolly mammoth, stupid," but we already know what the gun should be used for. Our caveperson is simply shaping the business model to the tool and not the other way around.

Eventually, the novelty wears off or he runs out of bullets, and soon the gun becomes a signpost. Our caveperson loses his popularity and the "elephant gun" market plummets. Was it up to the caveperson to be a good businessperson and use the elephant gun to shoot his own mammoth all alone and become "wealthy" in the eyes of his fellow tribespeople? Who is to say? The point of the story is, without keeping a clear eye on all four of the principles drivers of business, steering any business to success will be an iffy proposition, whether it is hunting woolly mammoths or running an "e-business."

▶ Taking the Plunge

How does this example relate to real businesses in the real world? The approach to be employed in this book is to identify the drivers, investigate the relationships among the drivers, and then use the drivers to extract some fundamental principles of e-business. These principles will then be used to nurture and develop a framework that is relevant to e-business strategies. It will become evident that e-business and e-commerce are successful only in the context of an integrated approach. A technology-only approach will not work no matter how powerful the technology.

Enough has been published on the definition of e-business and the differences between e-commerce and e-business. In our observation of the e-world, we have developed models and definitions for e-business and e-commerce and their subcategories. While we felt it was important to distinguish them, our criterion was mainly focused on the degree of change the different categories of e-business/e-commerce imparted on organizations. Throughout this book, we use the words "e-business" and "e-commerce" loosely, often interchangeably.

To build a set of principles and a framework for e-business, this chapter discusses the fundamental forces that are driving the e-business phenomenon. The focus is holistic—we look at all the basic building blocks, namely business, people, process, and technology. We observe that with disruptive technologies like the Internet and wireless, it is very important to approach e-business with an integrated view, and think in terms of all the basic building blocks in parallel rather than serially. The four fundamental forces have also become so intertwined that it is often hard to distinguish which driver belongs to

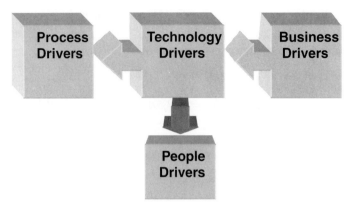

Figure 1–1   The original model and its four fundamental forces

which category. The old way of thinking looked like Figure 1–1 (not necessarily in sequence).

Our proposed model looks like Figure 1–2.

It is usually pragmatic to start with one driver (usually the business driver), but a sound business strategy needs to be developed in parallel from the very start. As depicted in Figure 1–2, the four primary building blocks are overlapping more and more with increased connectivity

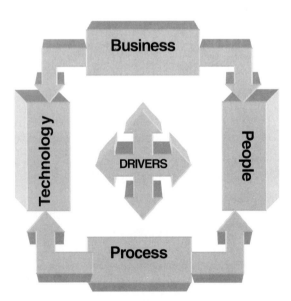

Figure 1–2   The four primary forces of our new model

to technology, but also from the business impact of the process, business, and people perspectives. These are the four building blocks that have the most impact on the "New Economy" organization.

We should interject here that any business strategy devised, even with the 4D Framework, will fail without a full understanding of the current economic playing field. One does not build a boat unless one knows whether it will be used to cross a river, a lake, or an ocean. The financial conditions today are drastically different than just five years ago with varying opinions about just what those differences are. Simultaneously, we find ourselves in the "New Economy," or "Knowledge-Based Economy," or "Internet Economy." By whatever description you call it, technology has fundamentally affected the world economy forever. Experts are still determining the overall impact to all of us, but that is well beyond the scope of this book. For our purposes, we will focus on the economic conditions and realities of what we will call the "Net Economy."

The Net Economy has been created by new technologies, the skills and knowledge of people using these technologies, new and ever-changing business processes made possible by these technologies, and, of course, the defining and redefining of old businesses and new businesses focused on these technologies.

Figure 1–3 illustrates this point very well. The value creation in a Net Economy is a combination of the forces of all four building blocks. Here, the opportunity creation results in business value creation; customer attraction and retention create people value, and operational efficiency adds to process value creation. All of them combined create effective value creation. The technology building block is implicit in this diagram.

It is still too early to tell where the Net value curve is heading. In the recent past, growth rates of technology companies were as high as 60 percent, but recently these growth rates have slowed down considerably, creating the first economic downturn in 10 years—but a downturn like no other. The forces of optimism and pessimism both have clear-cut grounds on which to base a conclusion on the immediate and distant future of our economy as a whole. That may be beneficial as we develop sound business strategies for a less certain future, but build safeguards for future downturns while factoring in results for possible upturns.

As the 4D Framework is introduced, the realization of this fuzziness and fusion in the real world of e-business is emphasized. The basic

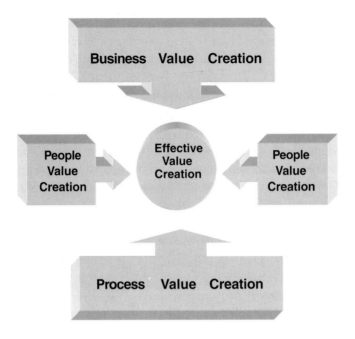

Figure 1–3   The Net Economy

building blocks are fused to give exponential value creation to the customer (see Figure 1–4). The multiplicative nature of these forces is clearly evident in this figure.

The multiplicative nature of these four forces (drivers) can be expressed in terms of an equation for customer value creation effectiveness:

Customer Value Creation Effectiveness = (B+T+P+Pr)

where:

B = *Impact of the business drivers*
T = *Impact of technology drivers*
P = *Impact of people drivers*
Pr = *Impact of process drivers*

But how can we use this formula in a real business using real dollars and cents? We'll use the first of many theoretical case studies to clarify the concepts of the 4D Framework. Let's start with the mythical YXZ Widget Manufacturing Company:

YXZ manufactures several different kinds of widgets and uses various components from outside vendors to manufacture each type. They must buy these components ahead of time to ensure ample supply and must keep a regular inventory of completed widgets to meet unexpected demand, if any.

The YXZ manufacturing process suffers from inefficiencies because of changes in demand. For example, YXZ produces the Type A widget and the Type B widget in equal proportions, since the market demand, on average, is equal for both. However, Type A widgets are made of iron and Type B widgets are made of steel and steel is roughly twice as expensive as iron. So at the beginning of each month, YXZ purchases a half-ton of steel for $1000 dollars and a half-ton of iron for $500. It then produces 1000 steel widgets and 1000 iron widgets. They then sell 900 steel widgets to their distributors for $1.10, 900 iron widgets for 60 cents, and keep 100 of each as inventory just in case. This gives them a gross profit margin of $180 for steel and iron widgets, respectively. However, they do have 100 steel widgets, which could be sold for a $10 dollar profit, and 100 iron widgets, which could be sold for a $5 profit. YXZ must swallow $15.00 when this inventory sits on the shelf. Fortunately, widgets are seasonal, with steel widgets selling well in the spring and fall and iron widgets selling well in the winter and summer. By the end of the year, their inventory is all sold off.

This is life in the "Old Economy."

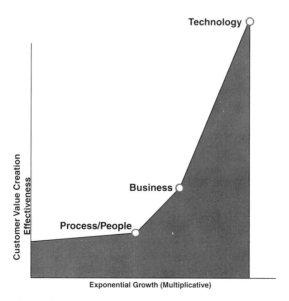

Figure 1–4   Customer value creation effectiveness

To move YXZ forward into the Net Economy, suppose the new chief technology officer (CTO) of YXZ Manufacturing has decided to go to a "just-in-time (JIT)" manufacturing system using Internet technology at its core. This means YXZ can now use the Internet to do the following:

1. Know exactly how many widgets are needed by using the customer site to preorder exact amounts.
2. Use a vendor intranet to order the exact amount of supplies needed to produce that order.
3. Eliminate the need for inventory.

In addition, widget supply descriptions can be fed directly into the automated e-design system so both iron and steel widgets can be made simultaneously without having to "refit" for one type of widget or another. This reduces overhead considerably and is much less labor-intensive. Now, let's take a look at our Net Economy drivers and numbers.

Business—Reduce Inventory/On-Demand Product Personalization

Since widgets are manufactured "on-demand," there is no longer a need to create an inventory of 200 extra widgets. This extra $15 can be seen as savings, added into gross revenue.

Process—Skilled Labor/Technology Specialists

It now takes an assembly line worker/supervisor who has some knowledge of the new intranet/supply/e-design system, and he or she needs additional training at a one-time cost, plus an additional $5 dollars an hour for an 8-hour day. If each worker produces one order per day, the additional $40 is easily offset by the $105 dollars the technology saves. YXZ is still ahead $60 per order.

Process—Applying Skilled Labor with High-Technology Processing Systems

The process of combining the $60 saved by "upgrading" labor and technology with the $15 dollars savings in inventory means a net of

$60 per order plus the $15 dollars. For 1,000 widgets we save a total of $60,015.00!!!

Of course, these numbers are hypothetical and based on ideal assumptions, but the point should be clear. **Small incremental value savings, mean a lot when aggregated.**

Technology—Intranet Order/Supply Systems/E-Design Technology

Because the new intranet/supply/e-design system reduces refitting time by, say, 3 hours, where each hour costs $35 dollars of skilled labor, $105 dollars is now saved per order.

Of course, this example is not only mythical, it leaves out a considerable number of other "real-world" factors the average business must deal with, such as marginal and unit costs of production and overhead, distribution costs, taxes, etc. But we believe the point is made. There are real economic advantages that the Internet and other technologies do add to a business, provided they are integrated thoughtfully into the core business. With that in mind, let's take a look at each of our drivers in more depth.

▶ Business Drivers

The different business forces that are driving the e-phenomenon are shown in Figure 1–5.

To Do Business All the Time

Many past major inventions—circular wheels, the steam engine, railroads, the automobile—have contributed to making great progress in trade and commerce. Then, theoretically, the e-design radio and television could connect the word electronically but it costs money to build broadcast radio and television stations. A lot of money. However, e-connectivity via the Internet has done what was simply not possible to do by other vehicles: It connected nearly the whole world in an easy, efficient, timely, and inexpensive fashion.

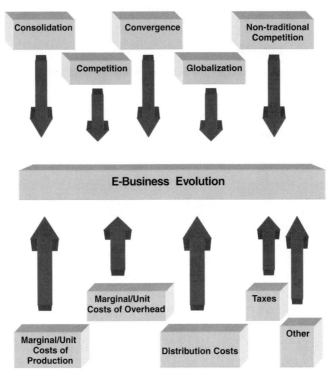

Figure 1–5   Business drivers

One of the early adoptions of the Internet by a mass audience was email. Email alone changed the landscape of global communication in a mind-boggling way. What used to take months, or even a few years in some countries, now takes minutes and the communication devices are so inexpensive that even economically depressed communities have access to them.

Therefore, the Internet enhances and supports business all the time, practically everywhere. Geography and time barriers are suddenly gone; in fact, time differences can be used very effectively to create continuous operations in manufacturing, programming, call center management, and customer service.

We have included the need for ubiquitous business as one of the business drivers; however, it is evident that technology is a very important component that catered to that need and may have even created it. The processes and people to support such businesses and technologies are also very closely tied together.

Figure 1–6 illustrates the acceptance of different technologies and shows how the e-phenomenon has been widely accepted worldwide to cater to business needs.

To Do Business Affordably

Efficiency, specifically cost efficiency, is usually the focus of businesses. However, according to Michael C. Jensen:

> Value creation does not mean succumbing to the vagaries of the movements of a firm's value from day to day. The market is inevitably ignorant of many of our actions and opportunities, at least in the short run.[2]

During the days of business process reengineering (BPR), one of the main objectives was to reduce handoffs, which resulted in decreased cycle time and less overall cost. In many business processes, this reduction e-designer stood in the way of increased inventory turns and decreased labor. The e-phenomenon, when properly harnessed, enables businesses to operate in a very cost-efficient way, without costly and

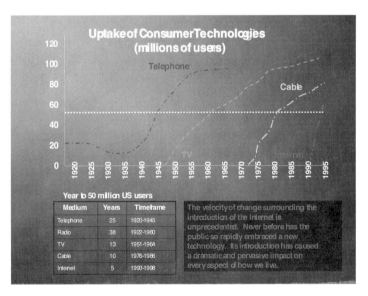

Figure 1–6   Uptake of consumer technologies

2. Jensen, Michael C., "Value Maximization and the Corporate Objective Function," Harvard Business School Paper: 00-058.

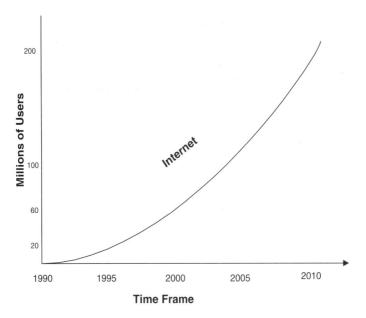

Figure 1–7 Illustration of the e-phenomenon's acceptance

dramatic reengineering processes such as the example described earlier (Figure 1–7).

The pursuit of cost reduction as a means of increasing operational effectiveness is particularly pronounced in certain products and industries. The distribution costs of anything digitized (e.g., software, music, video) can be very minimal. The Internet provides a very convenient, cost-effective way of distributing these products.

Generally, any adoption of software, whether packaged or custom, is an expensive proposition. Because the Internet is based on an "open" standard, the costs of application development can be drastically reduced. Any expense is generally in the knowledge base of designers and developers and not necessarily in the software itself. For example, Java is free to anybody who knows how to use it. However, complex application environments and platforms have demanded premium dollars. As the Internet development industry matures as a whole, these costs will steadily decline as well.

According to Michael C. Jensen, "Purposeful Behavior requires the existence of Single Valued Objective Function."[3] Reducing inventory,

---

3. Jensen, Michael C., "Value Maximization and the Corporate Objective Function," Harvard Business School Paper: 00-058.

or increasing inventory turns, is one of the main goals of business. Inventory can be reduced via several business models and operational efficiencies such as JIT, pushing inventory to suppliers, outsourcing warehouses, and efficient use of warehousing and logistics. Many companies are trying to reduce inventory by using the Internet and online shopping. Dell is a prime example of a leading company that has used online ordering directly by customers to reduce inventory significantly via accurate forecasting and super-efficient supply chain processes.

In the business-to-business (B2B) world, electronic catalogs are reducing costs in several ways. The distribution and printing expenses of catalogs are minimal; the associated cost of selling is also minimized. Complex procurement systems can interface with electronic catalogs and do fairly complicated configurations and pricing. This saves costs on both sides—the buyer and the supplier—in terms of labor, cycle time, and ease and volume of use. In addition, new information-passing technologies such Extensible Markup Language (XML) and electronic data interchange (EDI) allow expanded data interchange across the Internet, regardless of what permanent repositories and databases this information is stored in. In this way, disparate companies can exchange data in a universal format without the costly and cumbersome porting projects required in the past.

As these technologies take root and J2EE, .NET, and other advanced Internet programming technologies mature, doing business via the Internet will become as commonplace as doing business over the telephone. In fact, once data exchange across the Internet becomes standardized, Web technologies will be more ubiquitous than the telephone. The same data can be simultaneously sent over broadband, wireless, satellite, and even plain, old-fashioned telephone lines.

▶ The Net Economy Meets the Global Economy

The global village is truly coming to be a reality. While governments are trying to find new rules for taxation, customs, and security, the forces of globalization are continuing to dominate the Internet. According to Forrester Research, the rules of the Internet Economy are as follows:

1. Customer service eclipses the product.

2. Real-time demand drives production.

3. Pricing matches market conditions.[4]

Essentially, this model of business on the Internet is based on the relatively new idea of a network economy based on both "richness" and "reach." In traditional network models, being able to reach a mass audience usually meant an inability to customize any function for smaller or even individual portions of the network's customer base. Television, cinema, and telecommunications rely on sheer volume to make their numbers. Demographics and content targeting help, but out of three million people who watch the same commercial, only about 10 percent take any serious interest in the product being offered. The ideal would be to have all three million people see precisely the commercial on the product they would be interested in, whatever their individual interest. In other words, instead of driving the product to the customer, let the customer drive the product he or she wants.

Although this promise has yet to be fully realized, even on the Internet, the following business dynamics described in the following sections are becoming a reality right now.

Global Competition

Competition is now unrestrained. The barriers to enter an e-business have been somewhat reduced: information is readily available, resources are available via communities and intermediaries, and communication is almost instantaneous. The velocity of new entrants is often mind-boggling. The marketplace is also behaving like the stock market, auction-oriented business models are getting popular, fixed pricing is being challenged, and price differences due to geography are fading away.

4. Forrester, "Dynamic Trade: Rules for the Internet Economy," Netrepeneur meeting at the Morino Institute, March 1999.

Non-Traditional Competition

The Internet is giving opportunity to all and in very different ways. Since the barrier to entry to most businesses is lower because there is very little cost associated with using the Internet, it is easier for one type of business to get into other types of businesses. Banks are becoming investment brokers, and vice versa. Booksellers are not only selling CDs and other products, but they are also becoming auctioneers. The classic example is Amazon.com, which sells books, CDs, hardware tools, software, and more. Amazon.com is also aggressively pursuing auctioning. So, the traditional question, "What business are you in?" is taking on new meaning. It is also a debatable business model: Is this model sustainable long-term, or is it just an experiment of a new world that will ultimately fizzle away?

Communities

The Internet is providing the infrastructure of a true electronic bazaar. Communities-of-interest are cropping up and a very different set of rules for interaction is being established. These communities are interacting with each other, exchanging information, and generating value. Chat sessions, electronic billboards, and Web meetings are powerful tools that are giving communiti¬es the information they need, when they need it. Communities are also creating a strong market demand for products and services. For example, there are investment communities, engineering communities, sales communities, and project management communities that help foster communication among people with common interests. There are portal sites that bring certain ethnic communities together; for example, Satyam infoway has a portal (*www.satyam.com*) that brings the Indian community together to share their interests and ideas, regardless of their geographic location. There are similar portals for all social groups, religions, ethnic groups, and so on.

The dynamics of these communities and their influence on markets, on the purchase of products and services, and in bringing social changes have yet to be understood fully. However, their impact seems to be quite profound.

In the Old Economy, capital and labor drove the economy according to the following equation:

$E\,ff = (Labor + Capital)$

This gradually transformed into the equation:

$E\,ff = (I\,sn\,*\,H)$

where I stands for information and knowledge through social networking and H represents human skill sets.

The Internet is defining economic efficiencies in terms of this equation:

$E\,ff = (I\,dn\,*\,H\,*\,T\,ff)$

where $I\,dn$ stands for information and knowledge through social and digital networking, H represents human skill sets, and $T\,ff$ is for technology effectiveness. It is evident that digital communities are playing a major role in e-business.

Channels

In the initial wave of e-business models, people argued that the Internet would eliminate different "brick-and-mortar" channels and intermediaries and pass on the savings to customers. While this is true in certain industries, this has not always been the case. E-commerce intermediaries are becoming an industry by themselves. In either B2B commerce or business-to-consumer (B2C) commerce, there is a need for a complete solution. With the proliferation of products and services over the Internet, it makes sense to have some kind of solutions provider that gives value in terms of cost, efficiency, and quality. Cyber-mediation is providing this solution. For example, an Internet-based escrow company (*escrow.com*) is providing compelling value to a lot of e-sellers, especially from auction sites. In fact, all the portals like America Online (AOL) or Yahoo! are some sort of intermediary. The Old Economy intermediaries are also rushing into the Net Economy and providing value through meaningful aggregation.

Chapter **1** l Drivers of the E-World

Real-Time Demand and Supply

The availability of real-time data from internal sources like inventory and external sources like competitive pricing is creating a real-time demand/supply model, leading to price variations almost like the stock market. Companies are using auction strategies that are challenging fixed pricing. For instance, Sun recently introduced auction pricing on certain product lines.

New business models are emerging that allow prices to change in real time; for example, vending machines that vary price based on external temperature, season, or time of day. Forrester Research calls this mode of trading and price determination *dynamic trade*.

Auctions

The above discussion leads to online auctions. The online auction is a multi-billion-dollar market and growth is exponential. There are two types of auctions prevalent over the Internet. The English auction, where open bidding starts with a lower price and the highest bidder is the winner is the most popular model. Most e-auctioneers like eBay do this low-to-high bid-type English auctioning. Reverse auctioning is just the opposite—it starts with a high bid and then lets the bidders bid down the price. The lowest bidder gets the deal. This is a good model for vendors bidding for a contract.

Auctioning is becoming a part of the business model of most companies selling over the Internet. It seems to be the closest approximation of a free-market economy as we see markets getting closer to "perfect information."

Several companies started auctioning their own products via the Web. One of the pioneers in product auctioning was Sun Microsystems, when they announced this in September of 2000. CEO Scott McNealy signed a few limited edition Sun Blade 1000 workstations to hit it off.

Buying and selling products or services via English and reverse auctions have become extremely valuable vehicles for companies. Choosing to sell an item or service by auctioning it off is more flexible than setting a fixed price. It is also less time-consuming and less expensive than negotiating a price.

▶ People Drivers

People Make the World Go Around!

"Choice" is a powerful word. Disruptive technologies like the Internet and mobile and wireless technologies are giving choice to customers. Customers can get almost everything globally with competitive pricing and bids from the comfort of their home. For example, customers can get insurance information, shop for insurance, compare prices, and buy insurance in a few hours, sitting in front of a Web-enabled device. The device can be a terminal or other smart device.

Information is power. Multidimensional information flow and communication have given customers what they really want—choice. Powerful communities-of-interests are creating Web lobbies for products and services. Real-time prices, auctioning, and the power of information have enabled customers to use the Web as a vehicle to create communities with common interests. There are now multidirectional communication and information flows between product and service providers and customers. These benefit both buyers and sellers.

In the words of John McCarthy, Group Director of New Media Research at Forrester, "dynamic trade . . . [is] leveraging technology to satisfy current demand with customized response."[5]

Companies are getting powerful demographic and behavioral information in real time; at the same time, customers are influencing companies to provide quality, products, and services at the right time. The definition of quality has gained more dimension also. It incorporates traditional quality, speed, interconnectivity, and community experience on top of core products and services. (See Figure 1–8.)

Industrial economies were built on the *mass production* business model. Companies built products and "pushed" those products using one-way communication (advertising and mass media) to markets. Enabled by the totally interactive medium of the Internet, consumers

5. McCarthy, John, "Dynamic Trade: Rule for the Internet Economy," Netrepeneur meeting at the Morino Institute, March. 1999.

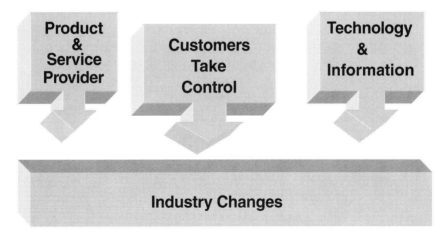

Figure 1–8   People drivers

can now "pull" the information they want about products and reach out to all sources instantly. This information is power, and it fulfills one of the tenets of pure competition, a fully informed consumer. "Fully informed" means having access to information from other consumers as well as information about the products themselves. What we see happening now is the slow change from the economic model of "economy of scale" to "economy of focus."

The Internet Experience

The Internet is allowing a different paradigm of mass production called *mass customization*, creating a world where real-time demand drives real-time production. It is not only allowing an enriched customer experience via real-time video, audio, and graphics, but also profiling customers intelligently and creating customization on a one-on-one level. Buyers are given assistance in decision-making, from loan calculations to comparative pricing and a multitude of options, which can be used by the customer to come to a decision. Payment processing has become quite efficient and secure. Back-end order processing and delivery are also improving in quality and speed.

However, it is not just trade. Chat sessions, billboards, and Web meetings are generating a very engaging Internet experience. Formal and informal meetings are being conducted and are becoming popular.

Teenagers are hooked on AOL chat sessions. Mobile, set-top boxes, wireless, and voice over IP (VoIP) have started to add to the Internet experience. As it stands today, the Internet experience can be encapsulated in three sets of coordinates (see Figure 1–9):

- Mass customization
- Self-service
- Communities

Mass Customization

The concept of mass customization has been there for a while, but the Internet is helping materialize the concept. Organizations can analyze the buying behavior of individual customers by tracking their electronic interactions and produce the right marketing messages, products, and services necessary for these customers. The intelligent Internet can keep all the customer information, update it, and depending on the buyer's demographics, psychographics, or any other model used to analyze the customer, deliver the right solution to him or her. This will lead to not just owning the customer for a window of time, but owning the customer for a lifetime.

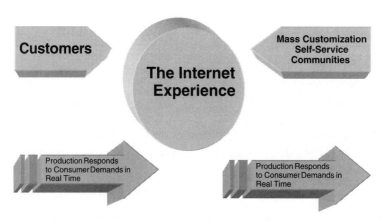

Figure 1–9   The Internet experience

Self-Service

Self-service on the Internet, if properly designed, can render great value to a customer. Customers will be empowered to track a parcel (e.g., package tracking system), resolve a technical problem, and perform other functions that would normally require human intervention and maybe numerous phone calls. If the site is properly designed and information is accurate, self-service can be a very meaningful experience for the customer and will be a win-win for both the e-organization and customer in terms of cost, experience, and time saved.

▶ Process Drivers

Transformed Processes

E-business is often about transforming end-to-end business processes. This means eliminating costs, reducing handoffs, effectively using resources, and creating horizontal processes that are aligned with the value chain (defined later).

E-business, especially transformed e-business (see the later definition), forces some very interesting process issues. Thomas H. Davenport states in his work: "In definitional terms, a process is simply a structured, measured set of activities designed to produce a specified output for a particular customer or market. It implies on how work is done within an organization..." He then continues: "A process approach to business also implies a relatively heavy emphasis on improving how work is done, in contrast to a focus on which specific products or services are delivered to customers."[6]

A business process approach is therefore a way of doing work that is necessary to add value for the customer and also all the links of the value chain. In the context of the Internet, business processes are taking two distinct perspectives: digital processes and traditional processes. As with anything else, there are mixed processes. A digital process is, for example, a Web-based ordering system that captures an

6. Davenport, Thomas H., *Process Innovation* (Boston: Harvard Business School Press, 1993).

order, authenticates the buyer, gets the customer profile, authenticates the payment, and places the order. A traditional process is the logistics part, where the order is physically delivered via mechanical means (e.g., a van). Again, nothing is a pure digital or a pure traditional process, but we are categorizing them as such at a conceptual level. In practice, the line is getting fuzzier every day.

The original BPR experts of 10–15 years ago had a vision in the right direction; they were cutting down the number of handoffs between people and divisions and reducing the communications barriers. However, technology was not as pervasive as today; emails were still new, mobile and wireless technology were very immature, and communication was costly. So, they had to make some disruptive organizational changes and often did it with poor communication and change management in place. This caused resistance throughout the organization. BPR also became a fashionable "buzzword" at executive levels, and top executives promoted their own selfish agendas rather than what was good for the customers and their organizations as a whole. This did not happen because technical managers were unscrupulous or unethical, but because the "closed" technologies of the past created "closed" internal economies. There was a buy-in, both technically and economically, around a particular platform, and usually the investment in terms of both dollars and time was considerable. Very few managers, once making such a commitment, wanted to change paths with another technology, even if it could do a specific job better, without some kind of a fight. In addition, since these decisions were made by a select group of "insiders," there was little accountability once the decisions were made.

The Internet is a great equalizer. The primordial forces are at play here. An email cc'd and/or bc'd to the right people holds them accountable in ways never before possible. A simple cell phone can cut down on hours and days of miscommunication—this can happen globally and literally instantly. Digital processes are changing work processes in a forceful, but nondisruptive way. The beauty of this streamlining is that it is not creating people resistance similar to what happened in the BPR era of the late 1980s and early 1990s. With open and effective communication, people (including upper management) cannot hide issues as much as they could previously.

So, the Internet has taken process transformations to a new level. However, the traditional processes and old handoff issues are still there. They have just taken on a new form. As shown in the previous example of Web ordering, the order taking, credit card verification, and payment transactions form the hyper-efficient digital process, but the order still needs to eventually be delivered via traditional processes. A perfect digital process can still reduce cycle times, but a handoff to a physical logistics part can still be broken. No matter how many orders for widgets are taken online, someone must still be notified to pack and send the boxes containing the order. Any bottleneck will lead to unacceptable delivery cycle times.

So, brick and mortar are not just going away. The new cliché is "click in a brick." Digital processes will coexist with traditional processes. Successful Internet companies have opened or outsourced warehouses (and logistics) and have integrated the warehousing and logistics systems with their Web-enabled order processing systems.

The dot-com bust is pointing to one very important lesson we all have learned: All aspects of business, people, process, and technology are critical for the success of any business. E-businesses have great potential only in conjunction with time-tested principles, methods, processes, skills, and sound business practices. E-hype is over.

▶ Technology Drivers

Connectivity

The fast pace of technical innovation has created a huge, amorphous mass that facilitates connectivity globally. Wireless, Internet, and mobile technologies are all converging and creating connectivity at the hardware and infrastructure levels, at the application level, and at the business level. Increased computing and communication power has led to the demand for intelligent products and services. Flexible frameworks/architectures tie all these products together.

The following is a vision often shared by Sun CEO Scott McNealy:

> Imagine being in your car on the way to a meeting and you can't remember the location. You activate your wireless device—your mobile phone or Palm Pilot for instance—simply by speaking. No

one else can activate your device because your voice has been authenticated. After a location search engine reports heavy traffic on the route you were going to take, it suggests an alternate path. You arrive at the meeting with time to spare and you could really use a cup of coffee. Your device directs you to the nearest coffee house and you make it back to the meeting feeling revived.[7]

While this may not be exactly what can happen, it shows the power of connectivity to enable a process and a business outcome. An important aspect of this connectivity is the creation of architectural frameworks that not only integrate Java-enabled handsets, Internet-based networks, and smart calendaring solutions, but older technologies like phone and fax.

This connectivity of infrastructures is forcing applications and business processes to integrate and align. Customer care, supply chain, and Internet markets (I-markets) are creating cross-organizational perspectives and forcing the creation of frameworks that can handle this whole fuzzy mass of "things."

The other aspect of this connectivity is the feasibility of creating new business models, new team-based and networked organizations, and cross-enterprise value chains. What this means in real terms is that technology has matured to the point that:

- **Anyone can connect anywhere, anytime**—This sounds like a cliché, but this is really what is happening. Information technology (IT) organizations are working very hard to put infrastructures, applications, services, and processes together to make this happen. The connectivity needs are 24/7, 365 days a year. Response times must be within tolerable limits, and applications need to be reliable and consistent in their behavior. Service organizations are talking about continuous service, continuous capacity planning, and continuous software change control.
- **Global markets and services**—Connectivity is cutting down all barriers to entry on a global scale. It is also allowing customer service centers and IT operations centers to take advantage of the time differences between countries and provide 24/7 service. The other effect of this connectivity is transparency. Best-of-breed products, pricing, and services (pre- and post-sales) are available to almost anyone who is connected.

7. Sun Microsystems, Inc., Web site, April 2000.

- **Need for systems, processes, and old-fashioned business backbone**—The new Net Economy needs old disciplines. Data center processes are becoming increasingly important. Teaming and project management disciplines are being reinforced. Just as client/server systems co-exist with and leverage mainframe systems, so will the newer Web-based technologies and systems integrate and use even older disciplines. Most successful e-businesses deploy this mixed strategy of Old Economy, brick-and-mortar processes with digital processes, hence the phrase, "click in a brick."

- **Intranets/extranets/the Internet/wireless/mobile**—All will merge into one big, amorphous mass and compartmentalization will become increasingly difficult. The whole e-world will become fuzzier than ever.

Anywhere

The "anywhere" aspect of the Internet has some interesting dimensions:

- Access to the Internet allows almost anyone, anywhere to have a Web storefront and conduct business. So, essentially, any business can be global in nature. In that way, the Internet is a level playing field.

- With barriers to entry reduced, capital investments are reduced because a Web storefront is not cost-prohibitive. However, any organization has to plan for these two aspects since the Internet can work as easily for the competition.

- The other dimension is that physical connectivity to the Internet can be increasingly achieved from anywhere. People can connect to the Internet via any device (mobile, wireless, etc.) and from "anywhere"—airport, home, office. These attributes form a fuzzy environment for business with extreme competitiveness on one hand, complex order-taking and delivery on the other, and a demand for goods and services in the marketplace that is quite unique. All aspects of business, people, process, and technology come into play. "Anywhere" is making the interactions between B2B and B2C much more complex.

Lightning Speed

Speed is at the core of the Internet revolution. New product introduction, time to market, ordering cycle times, and inventory cycles are all being challenged by faster and speedier requirements. Time is money, and reduced time means lower costs and greater customer satisfaction.

We know about JIT inventory—in the software marketplace, small releases are constantly being pushed via the Web as continuous and quick updates to existing products. JIT software releases are possible because of the Web.

Again, the speed gained by digital processes needs to go hand-in-hand with physical processes for the Web to be effective. That brings up the point that old-style process management and good overall process design are essential for both speed and productivity.

Convergence

The marketplace and customers are converging (see Figure 1–10). With the advent of mobile and wireless technologies—embedded devices and the Internet as the backbone—a global marketplace is converging into the Internet. Embedded devices in any product—cars, airplanes, refrigerators—can send alerts on possible product failures, the need for routine service, diagnostics, and so on.

Mobile workforces are being linked globally. PCs, TV, and telephony are all merging into the Internet. The possibilities are endless. The following scenario is often talked about:

> A refrigerator, which can detect quantities of food, does an inventory check and sends a grocery list, via the Web, to the grocery store. The grocery store automatically replenishes the food and delivers it to the door. This can be further extended by allowing the home security company to know when the grocery van will arrive to allow the deliveryperson to get in for an allotted timeslot via some secured entry.

However, under certain circumstances and depending on peoples' cultures and ways of doing work, some may not adopt such a Web order-

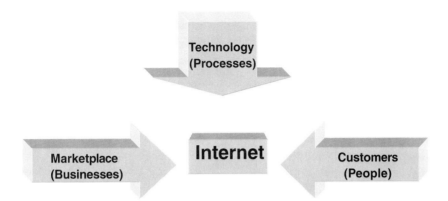

Figure 1–10   Converging forces

ing and security scenario. But the fact remains that the Internet has become a technology backbone where other technologies are converging. This will force changes in business processes, work processes, and individual lifestyles and thought patterns. Converging technologies are forcing convergence in businesses, people, and processes in both our personal and professional lives.

Why the 4D Framework?

▶ An Introduction to the 4D Framework

As we have already explained, the 4D Framework can be viewed as a four-dimensional matrix consisting of phases, building blocks, project management functions, and disciplines. Each dimension has four sub-elements, as discussed below. These dimensions have been created, studied, and implemented based on actual successful and failed e-commerce projects. In this chapter, we will assume that we are ready to embark on an "e-business project" of our own, applying the 4D Framework as follows:

- **Four fundamental elements, or building blocks**—Business, people, process, and technology elements are used first.

    The building blocks consist of these four elements. Elements can be tasks, methods, and processes themselves. The elements are flexible and extendible. The project team will choose from and may create its own case-specific processes/methodologies from those existing in the 4D Framework.

- **Four phases**—The phases comprise understanding, solution, implementation, and maintenance/monitoring.

37

Each phase has specific steps and checkpoints. For example, at the core of the 4D Framework is a continuous monitoring phase, where the e-project issues are constantly reviewed. These distinct phases constitute the 4D Framework.

- **Four foundation disciplines (the fourth dimension)**—The disciplines of high-velocity process management, value chain analysis, value chain linking/implementation, and change management are essential to identify, understand, solve, and deliver e-business initiatives. Of the four, value chain analysis, linking, and change management are the most neglected disciplines in many e-business initiatives. In this book, we have strived to emphasize and elaborate on these three disciplines in particular.

Why This Approach?

- E-business projects have decreased timelines, so super-structured methods do not work.
- E-business projects need more flexibility.
- E-business projects need to choose from a rich set of tasks, tools, and methods.
- E-business projects need a framework to contain the impending chaos.
- E-business project teams can create their own methodologies and processes as needed. For example, a typical high-level e-business methodology could include business architecture, technology architecture, and integration and deployment processes.
- E-business employs a balanced approach. It enforces a discipline that harnesses the creativity of an e-business team and focuses it for greater effectiveness. This approach integrates solutions with best-of-breed products, unparalleled service and support, implementation focus, and risk-contained migration plans.

The 4D Framework integrates all the aspects of an e-business's needs. It is the glue that brings all the tools of an e-business project together. It emphasizes solutions at the business level, architects technology infrastructures, ensures a seamless transition, and controls change management. It addresses not only technology, but is sensitive to all the other related drivers: business, people, and process. The 4D Framework is phased and release-driven; therefore, it provides for checkpoints at the end of each phase and also releases within a phase. As part of the approach, the team proactively assesses the business, applications, and data requirements and derives the right technology configuration in support of the organization's anticipated needs. This assessment is conducted with a professional project management discipline and involves various parts of the organization. The 4D Framework allows coordination of activities among various groups (company, division), business and technology consultants, engineering, competency centers, professional services, and outside vendors.

Explanation

We find the 4D Framework essential in conducting e-business projects. It balances the fast-moving, creative nature of e-business projects with some structure and discipline. It is structured enough and at the same time flexible enough to be productive. It lets the project team choose from a checklist of tasks, methodologies, and tools that make sense for a particular project. Each of the four phases allows the team to monitor the progress of each phase in a structured manner. It is also release-oriented and rapidly iterative. Since an e-business project is often a continuous process, it needs releases and deliverables that are continuously monitored and constantly reviewed. The idea is that the e-project team does an excellent job at any given phase and that the team does not need to revert back to the original phase and make changes. So once a phase is completed, it is completed for good (see Figure 2–1).

Most traditional methodologies emerged from structured development approaches centered on software engineering and other quality management systems (QMS) that were devised over the years to manage the development of technology and software. But, project management is project management, whether the project is for a simple proprietary order entry system or an extensive B2B procurement system. Most older strategies relied on coordinating step-by-step approaches to get many small tasks complete on the way to completing the overall

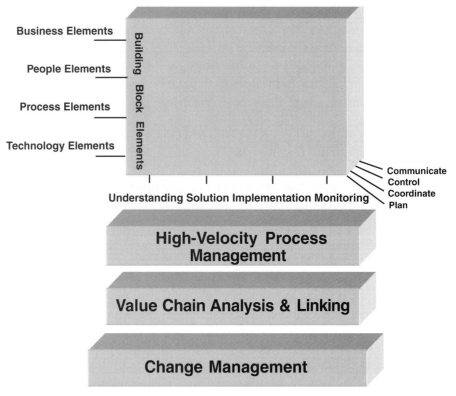

Business Elements

People Elements

Process Elements

Technology Elements

Building Block Elements

Understanding Solution Implementation Monitoring

Communicate
Control
Coordinate
Plan

High-Velocity Process Management

Value Chain Analysis & Linking

Change Management

Figure 2–1   Foundation of the 4D Framework

project. Waterfall techniques (see Figure 2–2) presumed that the results of one phase directly fed into the next phase. These methods got popular at one time because:

- They allowed the project team to control the scope of a project.
- They forced the team to do thorough planning and analysis at each phase.
- They worked in certain types of projects where project drivers did not change much.

However, waterfall methods were criticized for being:

- Too inflexible
- Too slow
- Too expensive

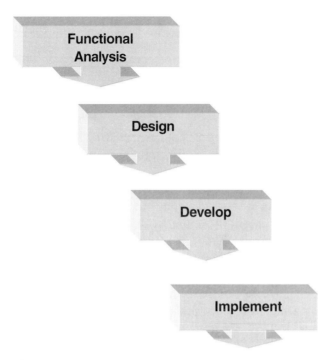

Figure 2–2 Traditional waterfall method

Additionally, technology decisions were often left out of future phases (which is nihilistic in an e-commerce context).

The waterfall methodology was traditionally applied to application development; however, the same approach may not hold true for e-business initiatives. E-business architecture, design, and implementation need to employ a spiral approach to technology projects.

Spiral/Iterative Methods Work Better

As the shortfalls of the waterfall method became apparent over time, people started to implement systems in general and e-business projects in particular using more iterative approaches. What that meant was that designers could go back and forth between different phases and modify older requirements or the design. This became a necessity as external social conditions made the business requirements and drivers change faster and faster. To aid this paradigm shift, processes and tools became available to make application development more iterative.

Spiral methods and all their different varieties recommend the use of parallel activities and adhere to a release-based approach. Each spiral encompasses a bigger scope each time to reach the ultimate goal of the e-business project.

In client/server or e-commerce projects, the process used by team members often combines visual prototyping and formal modeling tools. Modeling starts when the e-business project starts. Business event modeling is usually the first to start, followed by data and process modeling. But in an iterative methodology, none of this is done 100%. Instead, user interface prototyping is done almost in conjunction with the modeling. This goes back and forth several rounds to ensure that high-quality user requirements are gathered. Especially for e-commerce projects, the requirements gathering phase often uses use case methodology tools (e.g., Rational Rose) and inter-enterprise process engineering (IPE) to gather user requirements iteratively.

Thus, we see a clear trend of iteration across all phases of most non-traditional, non-legacy client/server and e-commerce projects.

In the 4D Framework, the spiral approach (see Figure 2–3) has been extended to organizational redesign. E-business drivers demand high-velocity, changing organizations. This necessitates that design and implementation be done in an iterative way—a typical example is creating an "organizational prototype." An organizational prototype is a small prototype of the new e-business—organization, work processes, reporting structure, communication strategies, and new technologies. This prototype tests the organization as a whole, measuring its performance matrix and spirally increasing the scope of control. Once these changed business processes are accepted, other business units are slowly brought in, tested, and rolled out.

High-Velocity Business Processes Demand Rapid Iteration

Today's e-businesses are under tremendous pressure to market products and services quickly. The Internet has reduced time-to-market

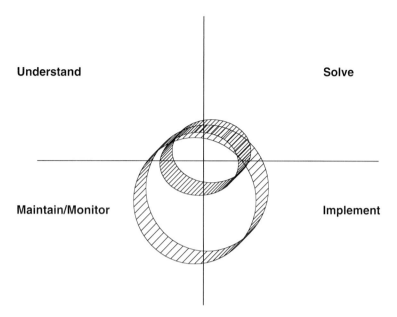

Understand

Solve

Maintain/Monitor

Implement

Figure 2–3   Typical spiral method

drastically and demands e-business initiatives to move faster than ever. It all starts with customers demanding the following:

- Products and services (high-quality, timely)
- Highly customized products and services (mass customization)
- A choice of price alternatives

The older waterfall approach worked for a while because customers did not have as much choice. End-users gave their requirements to systems analysts and "hoped" they would get a system that let them do their work. Technology projects were almost as inflexible as real-estate projects. Tools, techniques, and mindset were limited. Business-to-technology relationships were very linear (see Figure 2–4). What we mean by this is that business drove the whole show; technology was a child to the business driver. Customers demanded goods and services that created the business requirements and technology took a subservient delivery role.

However, this relationship has changed tremendously in the past few years. Client/server projects in the late 1980s and early 1990s started breaking the older paradigms. Coincidentally, the whole movement of

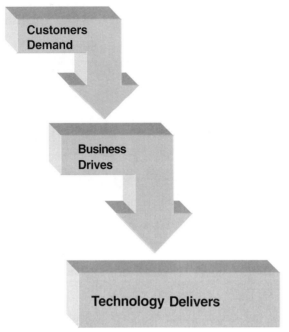

Figure 2–4   Business-to-technology relationship

BPR (even with limited success) forced organizations to think end-to-end, to think cross-enterprise, and to think like customers. Functional silos were criticized, though they were often difficult to break.

Technology has a greater, more dominant role of not just delivering to business, but also changing and modifying the customer expectations and therefore the business drivers. Actually this was happening for a long time, but now with the advent of the Internet, wireless, broadband, and more enabling technologies, the linear relationship has changed into more of a collaborative inter-relationship. This has resulted in a shift into parallel thinking, or systems thinking. Tools, techniques, and methodologies are supporting this parallel, iterative paradigm (Figure 2–5), where a simultaneous analysis of business and technology (application, data, and infrastructure) is needed, along with a continuing analysis of the relationships between people and process.

So, e-business projects are simultaneously technology- and business-focused, cross-functional, have rapid deployment goals, and are continuous initiatives rather than single-box solutions. A series of evolutionary product releases is often delivered to meet the time pressures.

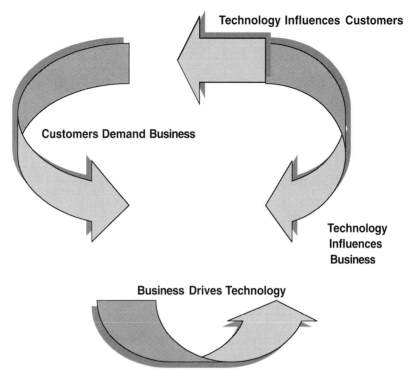

Technology Influences Customers

Customers Demand Business

Technology Influences Business

Business Drives Technology

Figure 2–5   Paradigm of the inter-relationships between technology and people and processes

This is even more relevant in the context of newer, more complex business models (e.g., English auctioning and reverse auctioning like the eBay and Priceline models), which are often global in nature. In fact, it is hard for e-business not to be global, not to be complex, and not to be under constant demand from customers.

Let's examine this with an example of an online procurement system. The business requirements necessitate the system to have several different use cases such as procurement from large vendors for computers and procurement of office supplies.

In a more traditional approach (there are different approaches, of course), the online procurement application would be broken up in terms of modules like sourcing, cataloging, requisitioning, payment processing, and receiving. Each of these modules would then be developed independently. Requirements would be gathered for each module, and the module would then be designed, tested, and implemented based on those requirements. This approach worked well in the past because of restricted customer demand, technology limitations, and lower expectations.

Conversely, the e-business project management approach is more functional, and depending on the size of the project, each module may have one project lead with all work under one program or project manager. There will be interesting problems that will crop up due to the lack of the overall end-to-end aspect of the e-business project. Additionally, the situation will be more complicated if the project is supposed to tie up with the order entry system of the vendor.

In an iterative approach, the design team will look at the cross-enterprise aspects (via IPE, perhaps) and end-to-end business processes—in this case, procurement processes from office suppliers and procurement processes from specialized vendors. The modules will be developed (or bought or rented) for each business process or use case using business modeling tools and techniques. Simultaneously, data modeling and user interface designs will be done in a very tightly managed, iterative loop. The application will then be released at an agreed-upon release date. This deliverable could be the end-to-end procurement process for office supplies. The next release could be the system to implement the procurement of large vendors. Again, this approach is very iterative, release-driven, and phased, as illustrated in Figure 2–6.

A quicker and smaller iterative approach is clearly evident, not just on the technology/business modeling side, but on the project management side as well. Future e-business projects will have extremely short cycle times. Release cycles will reduce to weeks, and there will be a need for what we call a *rapid-iterative* strategy to design, deploy, and maintain systems.

The trend is clear:

- End-to-end business process analysis and identification are becoming more critical and granular.
- Business-people-process-technology coordination is tighter and rapidly iterative.
- E-business project management disciplines are needed to manage this tight loop.

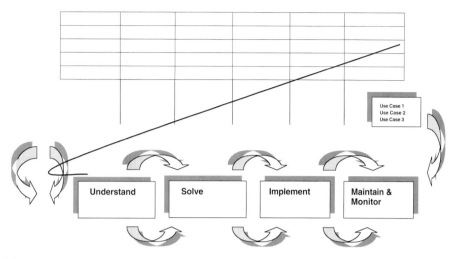

Figure 2–6 E-procurement business process

- Parallel and rapid design methods are increasingly required.
- Flexibility and designing for growth are critical success factors.

Most significant e-commerce systems are much more complex, much more global, and have many more demands to meet than the previous generation of client/server systems.

Some of the potential issues with e-business projects are:

- Global taxation
- Higher degrees of confidentiality and fraud protection
- Customs
- Government regulations
- Intellectual property rights
- Security
- Trust
- 24/7 availability

Some of these issues do not have regulatory solutions yet. This adds to the complexity.

E-Business Characteristics

- **E-businesses are more of a process than a project**—It may sound like a cliché, but "dot-com-ing" is really a continuous process. This is more relevant with the rapid changing of business and technology requirements and the demand for reduced delivery time for systems. By the time a system is delivered, its requirements have changed. Even if the functional requirements stay the same, the increase in volume and Web traffic demands continuous monitoring and a capacity planning process.

- **It is difficult to have a singular vision for tools, techniques, and methodologies**—Since e-business projects are cross-functional and cross-enterprise, it is often difficult to agree on one set of tools, packages, development methodologies, or even a single architecture. What that means is that a high-level framework of tools, methods, and tasks is needed. This framework must be a repository of tasks, processes, and methods to be used to create case-specific architectures and processes.

- **E-business systems will co-exist with and integrate legacy systems and processes**—Major corporations found out that legacy systems could not be totally eradicated. In fact, reusing the systems and processes and encapsulating them with objects (Enterprise Java Beans, etc.) makes more business sense.

- **Build/buy/mixture vs. rent**—In the 1960s, 1970s, and 1980s, building was the major strategy—either from scratch or by adding a lot of customization to a purchased software package. Development was targeted for a certain environment—IBM (or other) mainframes and some mini-systems or even personal computers (PCs) by the mid-1980s. Client/server and the availability of a whole suite of packages like SAP, BAAN, and Oracle gave customers access to buy commercial off-the-shelf systems (COTS). However, these packages often needed fine-tuning, and despite claims of minimal customization, the efforts were often substantial.

  Web-based applications have a very unique set of issues. First, they face the challenge of huge volume. Also, they have to scale to unknown limits. The Web is global; geographic locations do not matter. Application functionalities need to be delivered every

60–90 days. Neither the infrastructure nor the application can go down.

Web people skill set issues are becoming increasingly more difficult to manage. Therefore, there is a trend toward a rental Applications Services Provider (ASP) model, where you can outsource and just rent your applications. The pain of development, customization, and designing for scalability may be reduced, but then there are different issues that need to be handled. Service-level agreements, quality of service (QoS) issues, and managing performance via a well-thought-out matrix can be very complex. On the build-your-own side, the paradigm is shifting toward a component-based approach.

- **End-users and customers are more powerful than ever**—Successful e-businesses have customer-facing technologies, focused on existing and potential customers. A thorough understanding of customer requirements increases the stickiness (since e-commerce customers generally have low loyalty) and strives to make the customer experience as positive as possible. Customer buying behavior over the Internet is a subject by itself. Knowing real customers and their needs is so important because you do not have the customer in front of you. The customer can be from anywhere; location is unimportant. Market intelligence and understanding the customer's experience level with the Web are critical and having the smarts to influence that experience will provide the competitive advantage needed to succeed in the e-world.

Patricia B. Seybold, in her book *customers.com*, gives five steps to success:

- Make it easier for the customer to do business with you.
- Start with the end-customer's viewpoint.
- Re-engineer the customer-facing business processes from the end-customer's point of view.
- Foster customer loyalty.
- Use customer-facing technologies (kiosks, wireless, broadband, smart cards, etc.).[1]

1. Seybold, Patricia B., *customers.com* (New York: Times Books, 1998).

From an e-business project point of view, what this means is that e-business projects must focus on the customer issues and be built/assembled based on these issues. Customer and end-user involvement have become very important in the whole process of design and deployment, especially in building application prototypes.

Studying customer buying behavior over the Web, making the first contact with a Web site a pleasing one, and knowing more about the individual customer is a growing field that is leading to customer-service-oriented packages such as auto responders, online assistance, text conferencing, and others. Customer relationship management (CRM) packages are becoming popular as well. Decreasing order and delivery cycle times, increasing customer stickiness, and reducing overall cost will all be relevant if there is a 360-degree customer relationship that is well-established.

At the core of managing customer relationships is building some knowledge database using tools like analytic profiling, predictive modeling, mass personalization, and intelligent information broadcasting.

Keep the following in mind when building your e-business:

- **Understanding business requirements and customer needs is no longer a luxury**—Understanding the business is essential; in fact, it is critical in a successful e-business project. The influence and importance of technology is growing; technology understanding goes hand-in-hand with business understanding. A business model can be quickly verified and validated with technical tools. So, this forces e-business projects to understand the business requirements and validate them rapidly. You cannot wait until later stages to find out if the original business analysis was erroneous. You have to do this early on in the e-business project.

- **All the building blocks are essential**—The basic building blocks of e-business projects are business, people, process, and technology. They need to be applied simultaneously, iteratively, and in manageable chunks.

  For example, a portal company introduced a calendar, thinking this feature would increase traffic. They did not look deeply into customer preferences and psychology. The traffic did not change much. They already had weather forecasting objects in the portal, but in a separate place. When they surveyed their customers, they found that people would find it useful if weather objects (cloud, rain, etc.) were placed right into the calendar. So, here is a lesson to be learned—the technology was there, but people wanted to use it only in a certain, preferable way.

- **Good project management disciplines are a critical success factor**—The fundamental principles of project management are more appropriate than ever. Technology is helping to create a virtual team and facilitate project management globally. Since release timelines are collapsing, using sound project management principles and collaborative tools to create deliverables and measure the project against those in a much tighter loop are the keys to successful project implementations.

- **Cross-corporate collaborative teaming is important**—Technology is facilitating collaborative businesses like collaborative buying and inter-enterprise supply chain management. These collaborations demand cross-corporate teaming. This is beyond cross-functional teaming, which started a few years back. Often teams create different types of aliases and email groups to accomplish these collaborations. Ownership, security, and confidentiality all get very interesting when teams start collaborating on a global level.

- **Scoping e-business projects into small, manageable chunks increases the probability of success**—Internet e-business projects are best handled when they are scoped correctly and not executed all at once to do "total" and "drastic" changes to all the business processes in the enterprise.

- **A framework of collaboration, coordination, communication, and control is important**—Methodologies are great, but cross-enterprise projects often need a framework of methodologies and tools. Company A will most likely use different tools, packages, processes, and methodologies than Company B. The communication culture of the two companies may be different. To add more complexity, there will be more companies, vendors, and consultants involved. A well-structured program/e-business project office headed by a program manager and some project managers may help in achieving the necessary coordination and communication (see Figure 2–7).

- **E-business projects need e-business executives**—Executive support and the support of key players in the value chain are critical success factors. Since dot-com projects are strategic and touch all divisions, business processes, and outside companies, executive support from all the different companies is a must. It is a good idea to create an executive office to support and oversee the program office (see Figure 2–8).

Figure 2–7   A well-structured e-business project

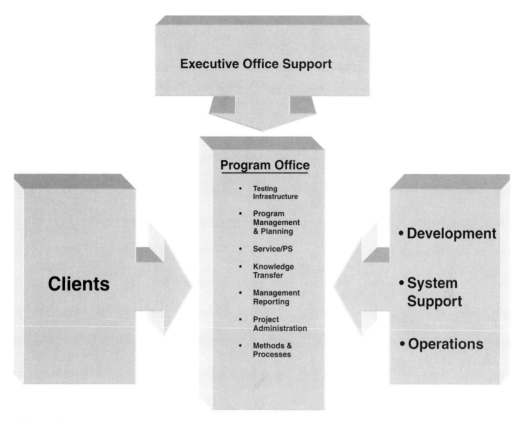

Figure 2–8   E-business projects need e-business executives

▶ Conclusion

The observations made in this chapter reveal the following critical success factors of e-business projects:

- Executive support and buy-in are required since e-products and solutions are of strategic importance to the organization. Localized management support will not be sufficient.
- You must have an understanding of your customers' business, people, process, applications, data, and technology needs as a

whole, and you must position e-business projects in that context.

- Often, organizational needs are complex and/or cross-functional/divisional/enterprise, which necessitates global team-building and a total understanding of the organization and its business processes as well as its partners.

- No single vendor, tool, or methodology can provide all solutions. Different integrators/third parties must be involved and the necessity of a framework is more important than ever.

- Since business needs are continuously changing, just focusing on current markets and paradigms will be a luxury. Engagements cannot stop at the end of one project; rather, a continuous program management approach must be employed. This will make the adoption of a flexible framework of business, people, process, and technology elements a critical success factor.

- The perception of e-commerce is that it is just servers, Web sites, broadband, fat pipes, and a bunch of running applications. This perception is far from the truth. The truth is, for a successful e-commerce implementation, business analysis, creative marketing, understanding global socio-economic issues, and the observance of a framework of tools, methods, and rules must be given the appropriate significance.

- Newer ways of doing business and high volumes of growth need flexibility, adaptability, and scalability in building and assembling applications. Simultaneously thinking about business, people, process, and technology and delivering solutions in manageable chunks are becoming the norm.

A framework that balances the principles of modern e-business project management with iterative development/deployment cycles using all the fundamental building blocks—business, people, process, and technology—is critical. The 4D Framework has been created with these objectives in mind. The 4D Framework is flexible, simple to follow, and at the same time, effective. It nurtures e-businesses with a total engagement process, from hardware solutions to Java architectures, from vendor management to getting consultants engaged, from business modeling to technology architectures. It is a framework that allows future plug-ins and adjustments. It takes into account business, application, data, and infrastructure. It addresses people, process, organization, and technology. It incorporates the disciplines of sound process management. It has different categories of tasks to choose from. It has more than tasks—it can also have processes and methodologies. To make the 4D Framework flexible, there is very little interdependency among tasks. A particular methodology under this Framework may introduce those dependencies, but not the 4D Framework itself. The 4D Framework addresses the needs of partnerships and collaborations that are critical with other vendors and describes methods to evaluate them and position them in an e-business project. It helps engagements change from a "technology-only" approach to a "business-focused, process-oriented, and technology-centric" approach.

The highlights of the 4D Framework are as follows:

1. Flexible processes, methods, and tasks
2. A holistic approach to business, people, process, and technology
3. Emphasis on phased and iterative approaches, breaking things into chunks
4. Sound project management disciplines

Part 2

Into the Matrix

The mesh between technology and business has always been difficult to define. Today it is almost as impossible for business to function without technology as it is for technology to function without business. Technology is usually expensive, although in the world of digital technology, the costs of both software and hardware have plummeted exponentially over the past 20 years. But still, the high costs derived in terms of time and effort still persist. It seems that the greater productivity introduced by new technology is almost always counter-balanced by the amount of effort it takes to master the new technology and make it work the way we want it to.

For this, there will never be a "quick fix"; that is simply the nature of the beast. But the world of e-technology does offer something that previous technologies did not—standardized design patterns across a network. The great business potential for e-technology is its ability for various organizations and individuals to distribute information and commit transactions across the Internet. The great technology potential of e-business is the fact that the systems used to do this distribution and commit these transactions can be created using the Internet. This may seem to add to the complexity of a project at first, but in reality, it makes things considerably simpler.

In the past, with insular, self-contained IT units, organizations were forced to rely on a core group of individuals to choose the hardware and software that the organization needed to rely on for years to come. The word "proprietary" began to creep into everyday IT vocabulary and because of it, more often than not, IT departments became political forums for the hardware and software of choice, easily losing focus of why all this was taking place—the need to satisfy a particular business need that only IT could meet.

If a department or division needed a new inventory system, too much time would be spent arguing about what or who would host it, what software should be used, what people already knew, and who needed training. Many projects were abandoned simply because IT departments would respond with either it couldn't be done, or if it could be done, it would cost a fortune.

As the Internet became the focus of IT departments, they were often forced to leap into the Internet world a bit unprepared, without being able to perform a complete and effective integration between the new Web applications and their "legacy" equivalents. Therefore, Web initiatives were often on their own, funded or sponsored by groups eager to have an Internet presence without fundamentally understanding why. It was simply the thing to do. Most organizations, even younger, smaller ones, realized that if their Web initiatives did not meet realistic business goals, and more importantly, mesh with their current technology investments, they rapidly became large sinkholes of capital without ever providing a return on investment (ROI) that could justify the money spent on them.

▶ The New Era

With the advent of PC technology in the workplace and the use of client/server technology to build distributed applications, organizations began taking a serious look at how to create applications that could deliver information and services to a variety of groups beyond their usual networks. At the time, most "network" applications were based on closed, proprietary networks like IBM's SNA and DEC's DECnet—both very powerful and reliable network protocols, but if you wanted to reach a remote customer via SNA or DECnet, that customer had to have an IBM or DECnet/VAX equivalent, respectively. Needless to say, these systems were expensive, so the cost of investing in such a network was high.

PCs and UNIX introduced the much less expensive worlds of Ethernet and TCP into network programming, allowing an inexpensive means of both developing and distributing network-based applications to anyone with a PC or RISC workstation. This was the beginning of "open" computing. Although the term "open" has many meanings to many people, for the most part, it means there is a set of technology tools that should work with a simple set of protocols and restrictions that, if adhered to, should ensure that each application using these protocols will run the same way regardless of the platform.

The Internet culminates the open era, releasing organizations from actually having to maintain and support their own networks. Anyone who has access to the Internet now has access to Internet-based applications. Still, organizations find it hard to translate all this new-found "convenience" into practical applications that meet specific internal and external business needs, partly because even with changes in technologies, protocols, and networks, the way people design and generate code is not much different than how it was done 25 years ago.

Although the infrastructure that supports e-technologies has been greatly simplified, that doesn't make the case for e-business initiatives. In fact, e-business initiatives are considerably more complex than the legacy-based, "proprietary" systems of old.

The complexity of e-business projects is directly derived from the fact that e-business projects are often cross-divisional, cross-enterprise, and global. There are daunting technical issues—build vs. buy vs. rent or a combination, integration with existing legacy and non-legacy systems, component-based development, Java and ubiquitous computing paradigms, planning for unprecedented growth, and around-the-clock availability and reliability. However, the business, people, and process issues are where the real challenges come from, and ironically, they are usually the most often ignored.

Old legacy systems and early client/server systems were very functional in nature—one hardware platform, one language, and one function at a time. It has been perceived that Internet-based technologies relieve some of the weight introduced by traditional IT projects. For instance, the simplest of models, adding "e-commerce" to a business, should require nothing more than creating a Web site that displays merchandise and accepts credit cards. On the other hand, e-commerce demands a multidimensional approach to designing, implementing, and maintaining systems. A buyer goes to a Web site, buys a book with a credit card, then what? Since a lot of e-commerce projects are proposed by business units, they often own them, or at least are strongly involved in their implementation. Therefore, they are inherently cross-divisional. E-commerce often crosses enterprise boundaries—a client's procurement system wants to talk to a vendor's order entry system as if it was an extension of its internal systems.

Business and IT managers are often in a dilemma as to what strategies, methods, and tools to choose. In most cases, they have to co-exist with the existing applications and standards already chosen. There is no one way of doing things. On top of this, end-customers and the general business community demand 24/7 up-time, resulting in a continuous design for more capacity and a reliable infrastructure.

These initiatives are not just for technology infrastructure and application development projects, but can be used for any project touching e-business transformations. So, according to the definition introduced in the last chapter, the framework covers e-commerce, e-business, and transformed e-business projects. The 4D Framework could be applied to a single project, multiple projects, a single initiative, or multiple initiatives. We are convinced from experience that a flexible, iterative, and continuous framework is one of the most critical success factors for e-commerce initiatives. Again, as has been already articulated, we will use the terms "e-commerce" and "e-business" interchangeably throughout the rest of the book.

3

The First Dimension: E-Drivers

▶ A New Definition for E-Organizations

Although our focus is the deployment of technology for Internet-based businesses and applications, the tools we employ can be for any kind of business that uses technology to do business. We have already examined the four principle drivers that should underlie any commercial undertaking. However, the list of e-drivers can be even longer. The four drivers we have already discussed describe the essential forces of the e-economy in terms of the 4D Framework. These fundamental forces can be generalized to develop a central idea on how to handle all e-business initiatives and should be the focus of senior management's strategic thinking.

It is also obvious that these four-pronged building blocks create measurable chaos in today's organizations and their structures, processes, strategies, and technologies. The older theories of work by Frederick W. Taylor, Peter Drucker, Tom Peters, Michael Hammer, James Champy, and many more are no longer fully applicable. Figure 3–1 gives a clearer idea of this concept.

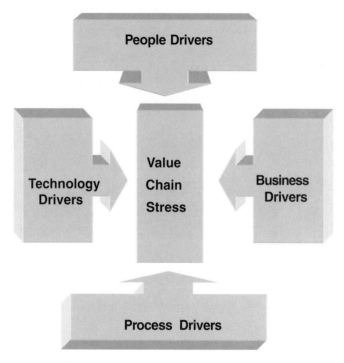

Figure 3–1 A new definition for e-organizations

To understand how these drivers interact with each other, and more importantly, how we can get them to work together, we must take time to understand how an organization works from within. How an organization and its various processes work from within and without defines the organization's "value chain." We will go into more detail on how the value chain affects any organization, and an "e-organization" in particular, in later chapters. But for now, we simply state that every organization's value chain is being stressed in ways that have not been experienced by corporate America before. This stress creates the current flux in the technology market since few businesspeople understand what separates past successes from past mistakes. Multidimensional forces in the Net Economy cause this stress; therefore, a multidimensional view is needed to provide solutions for organizations. This multidimensional outlook views an organization as an infrastructure, where the chaos of business, people, process, and technology is continuously evolving a model that works for awhile and then perishes. Thriving organizations are dynamic, creative, and fast-changing.

Traditionally, organizations looking for a more strategic position could build strategies on any one of the four building blocks. In e-organizations, we must consider all four business drivers in parallel, though we must prioritize and give importance to one or two drivers at a time. For example, in Figure 3–2, in the strategy-building stages, business drivers are given more importance than other drivers, but the other drivers are still analyzed and considered.

According to Figure 3–2, at the strategize stage of developing of an e-organization, business redesign, models, and market imperatives are the main "things" that need to be analyzed since they have profound effects on the organization's future directions. But, multidimensional thinking demands that we look into all people, process, and technology issues. Similarly, in the design stage, business processes are stressed, but other external processes are also considered. Eventually, the implementation stage will use people and technology will bring the organizational vision into focus. The cycle of strategize, design, and implement as applied to the basic building blocks is sustained in what we define as the "e-organization."

This above definition of an e-organization is very important because:

- It does not limit or define an organization based on structures and organization charts.
- It is not limited by any geography.
- It does not layer organizations into upper, middle, and lower tier (though such tiers may be needed), but defines organizations according to the basic building blocks and stages of activity.

Multidimensional Approach				
	Strategize	**Design**	**Implement**	**Transform**
Business	E-Business Transformation			
Process		Process Re-engineering		
Technology			Technology Redesign	
People				People

Figure 3–2   Multidimensional approach

This makes the layers of management independent of organizational definition and therefore gives organizations the fluidity they need to think "digitally."

- It creates a framework and grid that can be filled in as and when needed.

This organizational definition is therefore aligned with the needs of an e-organization in the context of the Net Economy, Digital Economy, New Economy, or whatever name it is called.

Levels of E-Organizations and E-Businesses

With the definition of the e-organization established, we need to extend that definition to classify and categorize e-business initiatives within such an organization based on how it should handle the four building blocks: business, people, process, and technology. For this reason, e-organizations have their own categories.

E-business and/or e-business initiatives are divided into three general categories as follows:

- **Transformed e-business**—These are e-businesses based on drastically new models or organizations that have undergone drastic changes to reach a new model. These organizations have a total fusion of business, people, process, and technology to create new organizations with disruptive business models. By disruptive, we mean models that can best take advantage of the occasional disequilibria in a chosen marketplace. It is when a market is in dis-equilibrium that opportunities for competitive advantage present themselves.

- **E-business**—This is a less non-conformist organization that reengineers its business processes using e-commerce systems and tools. The e-business is not necessarily looking for disequilibria, although it should certainly take advantage of any that appear in its chosen marketplace. This organization is simply trying to establish some kind of competitive strategy within an already well-defined market.

- **E-commerce**—There are two types of e-commerce initiatives: local and global. Basically, the organization is constrained to simply doing some sort of buying and selling on the Web. However, there is deeper pursuit of competitive advantage other than simply entering a new market and/or adding new technology to an old one. This type, more or less, is solely dependent on technology, but the other e-factors should still not be ignored.

We see that e-commerce is the first stage of Internet computing—simple trade and information exchange based on technologies that are loosely coupled and the four building blocks are not necessarily properly aligned. This is more of a traditional business with an "e-component."

We observe e-business as the next step up in adding value to an organization at a higher level, where business processes of different companies are integrated via enabling tightly linked technologies. This can be seen as more complex trades (e.g., B2B bulk procurement and order entry via, say, Web EDI) or more alignment between business goals and other building blocks. Processes are more streamlined and hopefully more efficient.

In the transformed e-business, all the components are in full gear and playing important roles in the organizational framework. Business, people, process, and technology are in unison, creating exponential Internet value (according to the formula presented before). New business models are formed, customer interfacing processes are streamlined, internal/external business processes are aligned, and creativity and deeper understanding of customers enable increased revenues and market capitalization. We have very rudimentary forms of these businesses in place today. Some examples of companies that may become transformed businesses are Sun, Yahoo!, and Amazon.com.

The following principles can be derived from the discussion so far:

- The Internet is defining economic efficiencies in terms of $E\,ff = (I\,dn * H * T\,ff)$, where $I\,dn$ is the information and knowledge through social and digital networking, H represents human skill sets, and $T\,ff$ is the technology's effectiveness. It is evident that digital communities are playing a major role in the e-business.
- All the basic building blocks—business, people, process, and technology—are equally important. However, the basic building blocks are getting fuzzy and intertwined. All four are getting tightly coupled. Connectivity in the Internet and Web is forming newer connections and new types of connections between business, people, process, and technology drivers.

- Quality, speed, and interconnection have generated a new value perception about quality (f = old-fashioned quality, speed, and connectivity). Speed and connectivity are creating new Internet experiences.
- Change management is fundamental. An e-business without a change management program has a high risk of failure.
- A fusion of Old Economy disciplines like program management/project management and New Economy speed will produce the formidable e-businesses warranted by the e-world. Phased, iterative approaches are integrated and fused. The failure of most Internet companies can be attributed to the lack of some of these disciplined approaches in program management and also undue trust in technology for the sake of technology.
- The speed requirement needs processes that are agile and high-velocity. This means processes that can handle quick demands by customers. They can be designed and implemented quickly and can handle digital-to-traditional (physical) handoffs smoothly.

All the basic building blocks need to be leveraged in parallel. So, holistic, parallel thinking is becoming important in any e-business, and especially in transformed e-businesses. Systemic thinking needs to be part of the core competency of e-businesses. This necessitates a discipline of thinking that aligns all the building blocks with an organization's internal value chain. Two later sections will describe the analysis and linking of important organizational building blocks.

Basically, this paradigm is not restricted to technology-based companies, but can be equally valuable to more traditional "brick-and-mortar" companies, whether they choose to embrace an Internet business strategy or not. The 4D Framework is designed to find and alleviate sources of "friction" within and between organizations. This friction is often created when well-meaning business initiatives find themselves at cross-purposes during implementation. This friction is sometimes foreseen, but usually it is not, thus creating unexpected costs and disruptions. For this reason, any and all initiatives should be examined very clearly using the 4D Framework lens.

4

The Second Dimension: Phased Implementation

The second tier of the 4D Framework (Figure 4–1) is composed of the phases required to define, build, and implement any e-business project. (For a view of the overall 4D Framework, see Figure 2–1.) Regardless of which type of e-business solution an organization chooses to implement, this aspect of the 4D Framework is probably the most crucial to success or failure. Without a thorough understanding of how one's own business works, its strengths and its weakness, it would be almost impossible to determine which strategies would have any kind of effect at all, positive or negative.

▶ Phase 1: Understanding Phase

Here we ensure that there is some basic understanding of the client (or ourselves). To gain this insight, we do a high-level assessment of the organizational directions, players, commitment to e-business, and the application and infrastructure requirements. The goal of this phase is to achieve a go/no go decision.

If the decision is to go, then some of the activities that make up this phase are:

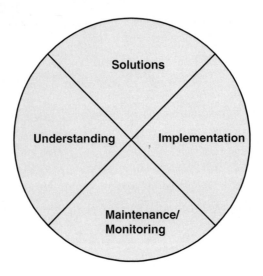

Figure 4–1   Phases of the 4D Framework

- Identify specific e-business projects.
- Understand the client's four fundamental building block elements and issues in detail. Build a holistic architecture.
- Establish and kick off a project team and develop a clear scope. Provide a detailed plan.
- Start some rapid iterative modeling using established tools and techniques. Create prototypes.

▶ Phase 2: Solutions Phase

The purpose of this phase is to determine the preferred solutions that provide the most benefit for the client. This phase will create a solution for the preferred process, organization, technology, and people requirements. It addresses the implementation and transition needs. Some of the activities that make up this phase are:

- Provide detailed architectures.
- Provide a primary solution (using, say, a buy strategy and one use case).

- Provide alternate solutions (using perhaps a combination strategy), if applicable.
- Develop a clear QoS agreement.
- Organize the project team, define roles and responsibilities, and agree on target release dates and deliverables.
- Provide an implementation plan.
- Provide a transition and training plan.

▶ Phase 3: Implementation Phase

This phase will ensure that the solution(s) provided and accepted by the client are implemented with minimal risk.

Some of the activities that make up this phase are:

- Reorganize the project team, define roles and responsibilities, and agree on target implementation dates and deliverables.
- Follow through the detail plan, which will ensure success of the implementation.
- Organize a smooth transition (this could be on a use case basis).

▶ Phase 4: Maintenance and Monitoring Phase

This phase will ensure that all the activities for the account project are well-coordinated. Work processes and how to improve on process efficiencies have been a subject of research and study from the dawn of civilization. In recent times, Frederick W. Taylor, Tom Peters, Peter Drucker, Professor J.M. Juan, Michael Ham.ner, James Champy, and others have done research and implemented their models of work process improvement, and redesign in various organizations. Each model has its strengths and weaknesses.

In e-business initiatives, whether we are dealing with local e-commerce, major e-commerce, e-business, or transformed e-business, the depth and breadth of process design will vary. However, the underlying principles and approach to e-business process redesigns remain the same.

One basic question that needs to be asked is: "Will the effects of the e-business change be drastic within the organization?" If the answer to the questions is yes, then it probably falls under the realm of e-business or transformed e-business and hence needs drastic process redesign. If the answer to the question is no, then it is an e-commerce-type project and so the process redesign will probably be more of a process tuning or small change.

The core objective of this phase is to ensure that a completed change becomes the new organizational norm. This includes not just the e-commerce components but also the other aspects, namely business and organizational change. A more ambitious objective is to encourage the development of what has been called *organizational learning*. The concept of organizational learning is the development of an organization that will be able to adapt and change itself as the external environment changes. For this to occur, the members of the organization must make the new vision their own. A successful monitoring phase will become in time a "bottom-up" process. As the organization adapts to the new situation, its members must be able to transmit information upward to facilitate the adjustments that will be required to the original implementation plan. So, the monitoring phase creates an environment where there is bi-directional change initiatives going on "bottom-up" as well as "top-down."

This phase allows the change managers to obtain feedback from the members of the organization. The change managers will then be able to adjust the detailed plan as necessary or to assist the members of the organization to adapt to the new situation. It is at this point that complex conflicts can emerge. Major conflicts arise between employees and middle managers, as often the vision coming from the top is not well understood in the context of implementation. There will also be conflicts at the executive levels and front line management levels. Another interesting phenomenon observed is that often hidden agendas blur the good intentions of change and change managers who want drastic changes may be viewed as disruptive. If the monitoring phase is omitted or incomplete, behaviors may seem for a while to conform to the new plan, but will eventually regress to old patterns of behavior and thought. One may also observe a "refreezing" of behavior at a superficial level of compliance, which is aimed at avoiding open conflicts, but may not be a sufficient level of commitment for the organization to reach its goals.

▶ Change Continues

Since there are typically different types of activities, outputs, and risks associated with the different phases of the change implementation process, this model can be used in a number of ways:

- When embarking on a specific assignment, it can help diagnose where a project is in terms of the change implementation process.
- It provides guidance as to the specific methods, activities, and requirements needed to move the change implementation process along to the next stage.

It is likely that attempts to "jump the gun"—that is, perform activities of one stage when the change process is at another stage—will have a high chance of failure. For example, attempts to apply detailed focused project planning and management techniques at the understanding stage will probably fail because senior managers may still have different views as to the nature and need for the change and because the required commitment and resources have not yet been secured.

Similarly, attempts to do activities of earlier phases in the solutions and implementation phases will probably fail because of the inherent interdependencies of tasks and activities and phases. This is especially true for when it comes to change management. Table 4–1 provides references to the key activities and outputs associated with each phase of the change implementation process. The guidelines describe the activities and concerns typical of a given phase, the symptoms associated with unsuccessful completion of a given phase, and the type of project management approach typical of a given phase. A more detailed description of the composition of e-transition plans will be presented in a later section.

In short, the activities and phases need to be followed as closely as possible and the process needs to be well defined and followed through.

Understanding Organizational Culture

The most realistic approach in understanding the change requirements of any organization is to consider that organizational culture exists, that it is a very core part of the organizational texture, and that, in times of change, it needs to be dealt with explicitly. This model is based

Table 4–1 The Process of Change

	E-Initiatives	Results Derived	Success Criteria
	Organizational diagnosis. Competitive analysis. Executive planning workshops. Executive change readiness workshops.	Mission, vision, and value statements. Case for change. Initial change agenda and targets.	Top team aligned with mission, vision, and values.
Understanding Phase	Cascading of mission, vision, and values to senior managers (workshops). Change process and readiness seminars for management. Development of new organizational architecture. Creation of organizational change team.	Architecture-level description of target organization, including new design and operations principles. Identification of core capabilities and critical business processes. Operational design criteria.	Buy-in from critical mass of senior managers. Senior managers act as sponsors, presenting and defending the project. Resources committed to change team. Change team reports to executive level.
Solutions Phase	Broader involvement of personnel through design teams. Information systems planning, process reengineering-focused project. Identification of and actions regarding quick hits.	Identification of different operational alternatives and choices. Design of process and systems (new and improved).	Critical resistances handled. Heavy involvement from middle managers. Overall detailed design coherent and complete. Middle mangers are most likely to be involved in this phase.
Implementa-tion Phase	Project development and management. Creation of implementation teams and program office. Implementation of interim management structures and processes. High level of communication and education.	Detailed implementation plans. Project management structure and processes. E-transition management structure and processes. Issue resolution mechanisms.	Good planning. Availability of resources. Adjustment to specific contexts and unexpected difficulties. Collaboration from line managers and working level personnel.

Table 4–1   The Process of Change (Continued)

	E-Initiatives	Results Derived	Success Criteria
Maintenance and Monitoring Phase	Set up transition teams and other feedback mechanisms for e-transition process. Change consolidation activities.	Continuous and persistent change.	Adjustments to proposed change made locally. Other organizational systems modified to support new organization.

on the fact that organizational culture has a powerful effect on the result of a change effort. Indeed, a change that is in line with the prevailing organizational culture involves less risk than introducing a change that is radically different from the prevailing culture. In the latter situation, if the existing culture is not altered, the change inevitably will not be successful. Organizational culture is defined as the dominant set of rules, roles, principles and values, and prohibitions that govern daily life within the organization. These rules, roles, principles and values, are the expressions of the values and beliefs on which individuals make decisions about the organizations goals, aspirations, relationships with other employees. These values and cultures guide the organization, especially during adverse situations.

This understanding supports the identification of the dominant culture of that part of the organization affected by the change and whether multiple cultures exist within the organization. It supports the definition of change by ensuring that major changes are planned to take advantage of the current culture. It also supports the evaluation of the feasibility and risk associated with a particular change and may help to identify changes to the existing culture required to support the change effort. Finally, it supports the identification of appropriate e-transition approaches, based on the compatibility of the proposed change within the prevailing organizational culture.

Maintenance/Monitoring Phase

Apart from continuous change and organizational behavior monitoring, this phase has all the elements needed to maintain the systems and further assist in the iterative design and implementation of future releases. In other words, the four basic blocks are never stagnant. They are constantly changing, technology in particular. Even with a simple e-commerce system, software is constantly updated from one revision to the next, business rules change as the business matures, and of course, new products may be offered at any time. Usually, most organizations deal with these issues as they surface, but the most effective organizations develop a means to deal with the maintenance as opposed to dealing with what needs to be maintained. This is vital to the success of any technology-based business and/or strategy.

Table 4–2 is a list of the most important elements of maintaining an evolving e-strategy.

Table 4–2 Elements of an Evolving E-Strategy

Building Block Elements/Functions	Tasks/Methods/Processes
Project management functions	Maintenance Plan (detail) Kickoff meeting Status meeting Roles and responsibilities Project status Communication plan
E-Business elements	Use cases ROI on processes (backup, DR, etc.)
Technology elements	Hardware/software integration Performance requirements Capacity planning Traffic analysis Systems testing Package tuning Service-level agreements (QoS details)
Process elements	Process (any) modeling Rapid/iterative methods Policies and procedures for maintenance Change management Software change management Disaster recovery process Data center policies 24/7 Web availability process Maintenance matrix (detailed)

Part 3

The Third Dimension: Redesign Disciplines

Now that we have a firm understanding of what the 4D Framework is and what it can do, we will now take a closer look at individual disciplines that define the Framework, how they fit together, and how we can use them to define and implement successful e-businesses. First, let's look at the four disciplines within the 4D Framework that, on their own, have been vital techniques in defining successful businesses for years:

- Value chain analysis
- Value chain linking/implementation
- High-velocity management
- Change management

▶ Value Chain Analysis

The value chain analysis analyzes the desired business, people, process, and technology outcomes/goals and also identifies the important e-business initiatives. Once the basic elements—value chain results, e-initiatives, and influencers—are identified, they are classified in a grid and the next discipline comes into play.

▶ Value Chain Linking

Value chain linking is a process/methodology to traverse the value chain of organizations and link e-business results with e-business initiatives. In the whole space of e-business and e-commerce, this is often a much ignored topic. Often, e-commerce initiatives are undertaken and executed without deep understanding of the "what's"—particularly what business problem they are solving. So-called e-business companies have failed because technology initiatives may not reinforce each other and may not be aligned to the business imperatives. Or in other words, they are lopsided; all four elements and all initiatives must be well-coordinated.

In this part of the book, we will particularly emphasize the disciplines of value chain analysis and linking. We have devoted the next two chapters to creating a methodology to do the business of technology analysis and linking.

▶ High-Velocity Process Management

The last two disciplines are *interactive* disciplines, that is, while value chain analysis and linking can take place at a very high level and generally, in the abstract, management is management. It is a day-to-day process that is as much of an art as it is a skill. The success of any organization can only be realized by the success of the individuals that comprise it, especially in an e-business.

Each individual in any busy organization, large or small, regardless of their title or status, is first their own manager. They manage their time, their work habits, and their goals. If their job title extends to managing, they must first learn to manage themselves before they can successfully manage others. As technology intertwines itself more and more into daily business activities, these disciplines must be intertwined with them. The final section of this book is devoted to this subject.

Digital process design is based on the same disciplines of any process design, be it manufacturing or a pure business process like order processing. The end-to-end workflow and the understanding, solutions, and implementation need to be high-velocity—many parallel tasks need to be done much faster to meet the ever-demanding needs. The interface between digital processes and traditional business processes needs to be very skillfully designed.

▶ Change Management

The other important subject dealt with in this book and in the 4D Framework is managing change. This change encompasses business, people, process, and technology. Most e-business projects almost blindly ignore this aspect, but our experience is that this needs to be institutionalized in all e-initiatives.

Value Chain Analysis

▶ Introduction

The previous dimensions of the 4D Framework were primarily concerned with understanding the nature of doing business in general and how to maximize an organization's value proposition. Now that we understand the basic principles of strategic positioning, competitive advantage, and value creation, let's take a look at how to actually make these principles come to life within both traditional and e-businesses.

The 4D Framework highlights four active management principles: high-velocity process management, value chain analysis, value chain linking, and change management. This section is an overview of value chain analysis, presenting a detailed description of what it is and how it leads to the subsequent value chain linking step. It provides techniques and templates to capture a pool of value chain entities; these entities express what processes create value within an organization and how they interact.

There are many views of just what value chains are and how they work, depending on whether we are discussing internal value chains or external value chains. Michael E. Porter first proposed the standard definition of a value chain as follows:

> Porter proposed that in most industries, firm-level value chains consist of five key activities—inbound logistics, operations, outbound logistics, marketing/sales, and service—plus the four support activities of technology development, procurement, human resource management, and corporate infrastructure.[1]

Generally, a value chain describes what actually happens in an organization that gets things done. It is more than just process analysis because it gives equal weight to the entities defining and carrying out these processes as well as to the processes themselves. But the traditional view of value chain analysis was confined to "brick-and-mortar" organizations. There are many scholars, professionals, and businesses that find value chain analysis readily adaptable to e-business "as–is," but for our purposes, we will take an entirely different view. For our purposes, there are four primary value chain entities: value chain results, e-initiatives, influencers, and the value chain matrix.

Simply put, four-dimensional value chain analysis is based on the principle that to do e-business transformations, an organization's value chain needs to be understood and the business, people, process, and technology elements associated with each level of the value chain need to be identified and validated. This identification and validation is done via internal and external research and analysis, facilitated brainstorming sessions, and interviews of the relevant business units and/or the corporation as a whole. The general idea is to get a first-hand view of just how the organization actually works.

The four-dimensional value chain analysis technique can be used as a standalone process/methodology to identify working value chain entities. It can also be used as a companion method to other methods of the 4D Framework to ensure that activities being carried out are focused on providing the desired e-business results. When used with other 4D Framework methods, it can provide greater impact to an organization's e-business transformation.

The key advantages of this method is that it can be used to:

---

1. Boudreau, John W., Benjamin B. Duford, and Peter M. Ranstad, "The Human Capital Impact on E-Business: The Case of Encyclopedia Britannica," in *Pushing the Digital Frontier,* edited by Nirmal Pal and Judith M. Ray (New York: Amacom, 2001), Chapter 10, pp. 192-221.

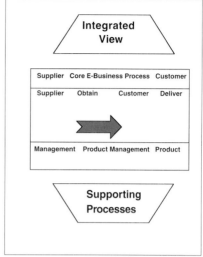

Figure 5–1   Digital transformations involving core e-business processes

- Identify e-business results desired. Before the value chain analysis level, there is no linking between the results, e-initiatives, and influencers. They are just put in their appropriate slots in the grid (discussed later).

- Help identify all the different parts of the organization that may be involved in e-business results implementation as well as the nature of the cross-organizational efforts required.

It can be used to support incremental as well as breakthrough thinking, goals, and objectives while looking at the best ways for an e-initiative to profit an organization, particularly those embarking on a major change, that is, becoming a transformed e-business. (See Figure 5–1.)

When to Apply the Method

The method is applicable when:

- A number of business processes need to be redesigned concurrently.

- Very limited time is available to complete the redesign.

- The digital transformation philosophy is already accepted by at least the top executives, even though they do not know which process to change.
- Data is not readily available to use in simulations to analyze process problems.

First, the "core e-business process" of the organization needs to be identified and defined; value chain analysis and linking may be used to identify this business process. The core e-business process identifies the key delivery and administrative processes that must be in place for a management team to run an organization. It includes the main products and services that the organization produces through its product/service delivery chain and support functions.

This method provides both "as-is" and "to-be" models of the organization using the 4D Framework. It can use all techniques available such as total quality management (TQM) techniques like fishbone analysis or any other established technique used to harness people's knowledge of the situation, rather than using simulation to understand the cause of the problem and to redesign the process to exploit or eliminate it. The same techniques are used where there is no existing process at all, and it must be designed from scratch.

▶ What Is a Value Chain?

Adrian J. Slywotzky, in his book *Value Migration*, postulates value chain as an outside-in approach that begins with the customer and works its way back.[2]

The value chain is the chain of business, people, process, and technology that links the customer to the inner workings of a company. This is different from an inside-out strategy, which looks at cost and quality only.

Remember, the value chain is the chain that links an organization's customers to the very operational aspects of the organization. It represents the different levels of any organization, its functions, and the interrelationships between levels. This clearly gives an overview of

2. Slywotzky, Adrian J., *Value Migration: How to Think Several Moves Ahead of the Competition* (Boston: Harvard Business School Press, 1996).

what the value proposition at each level is and how these value propositions are linked to each other to provide the ultimate service/product to the customer.

4D Value Chain Analysis

The four-dimensional method of analysis is founded on the principle that the context of an organization along with all the relevant drivers (business, people, process, and technology), are absolutely necessary to making e-business transformations. It has an associated technique that analyzes the value chain of an organization (or part of it) and creates three sets of entities:

- **Value chain results**—The results (business, people, process, and technology) that an organization desires to achieve.
- **Value chain e-initiatives (business, process, people, technology)**—Initiatives/projects/programs that are relevant and pertinent to the e-business context and produce the results.
- **Value chain matrix**—A two-dimensional matrix where the rows are the four basic elements (business, people, process and technology) and the columns are custom-developed based on the context of the value chain analysis (e.g., customer markets, products, services, etc.).

The 4D Framework-Value Chain Relationship

Value chain analysis is designed to support the other tasks/processes and methods embedded in the 4D Framework. It provides a framework for ensuring that all of the different actions directed by the other 4D Framework methods are value chain results-driven. It also provides a means for integrating strategy, business, and technology architecture/design and change delivery activities within a comprehensive program management framework.

Figure 5–2 illustrates the phases of the 4D Framework (understanding, solution, implementation, and maintenance/monitoring) integrated with the value chain program.

The value chain analysis technique is also linked to the following:

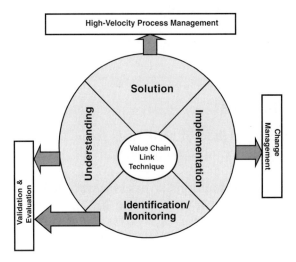

Figure 5–2   Value chain results management cycle

- Value chain linking techniques, which provide the techniques for determining the viability and value of an e-initiative and how it relates to the e-business goals.
- High-velocity process management, which provides a quick method of changing old business processes to suit e-business process needs.
- Change management, which provides an overview of the processes and techniques to identify, evaluate, integrate, control, and deploy changes associated with an e-business transformation.

One interesting and pertinent observation is that all these different elements of the 4D Framework are glued together via change management. Change management is a common factor to almost all other processes and initiatives.

▶ Basic Definition and Concepts of the Value Chain

This section outlines the inherent challenges as well as the basic concepts associated with the identification and evaluation of value chain entities, namely value chain results and e-initiatives.

Different Types of Value Chain Results

The in-depth analysis of numerous e-initiatives as well as the unpredictability of results associated with large-scale organizational change point to the difficulties of bringing about lasting improvements in organizations. One of the inherent difficulties with value chain results identification is that value chain entities are dynamic. They are functions of both subjective and objective views. An e-initiative can produce a range of results that can potentially represent viable value chain results depending on the way they are perceived on the individual level by key stakeholders. The perception of value is also largely dependent on organizational and environmental viewpoints.

Therefore, in addition to providing the means to identify and track meaningful results stemming from an e-investment as they unfold over time, we should have a multidimensional view of the desired outcomes and e-initiatives. This view should incorporate both the perceptual value (subjective and cultural) and objective value (financial/market-wise) attributed by the initiators as well as the agents of change.

In terms of value chain results implementation, the nature and magnitude of value chain results associated with an investment seem to be more dependent on the organizational context in which they are deployed than on the nature of the investment. The major issue is that value chain results are rarely the immediate results of an investment. Implementation is rarely determined by a sole e-initiative, but is usually achieved through a sequence of intermediary results that are often contingent on the achievement of additional e-initiatives and contextual factors that may not be part of the analysis. For the sake of manageability, we cannot tie every possible factor to a single outcome. This is, after all, high-level analysis, not statistics.

One requirement therefore involves the identification and management of all organizational e-initiatives as well as the organization's primary operational factors that can potentially affect the implementation of desirable results. These need to be explicitly managed to increase the effect of the e-initiatives to attain the aligned value chain results.

To address the inherent challenges associated with value chain results management, a number of key concepts are proposed which represent the fundamentals of the method. They are:

- Two distinct management cycles: strategic and tactical
- E-investment bundles

Two Different, Yet Integrated Value Chain Management Cycles

The four-dimensional values method makes a distinction between two different management cycles: the e-investment cycle and the value chain results management cycle are the embodiments of strategic and tactical cycles respectively. (See Figure 5–3).

The nature and magnitude of value chain results are directly related to the underlying e-investment, and e-investments will automatically lead to the projected value chain results. This tactical management approach focuses on a limited set of variables associated with the e-investment's delivery mechanism. Essentially this conforms to the idea that an e-business, like any other business, should seek an adequate long-term ROI. The purpose of the value chain analysis is to ensure sustained profitability, which generates real economic value. However, if responding to the investors' perceived desires is the only strategy, chances for long-term success are minimized.

The strategic value chain results cycle, on the other hand, follows a different logic. It states that the achievement of the desired results from an

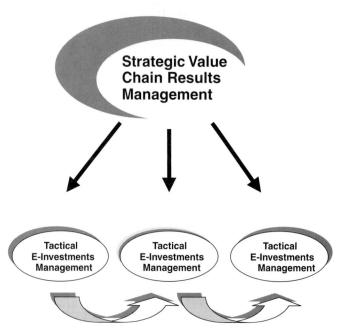

Figure 5–3   4D value chain results management

e-investment do not exclusively depend on the nature of the investment. Rather, it depends on a greater and more complex set of coordinated e-initiatives and internal and external organizational factors. Targeted results or goals are not assured. The nature and relevance of the targeted results or goals can change over time according to different stakeholders' perception and knowledge as well as one's understanding of the continuous changes in the organization's internal and external context. In other words, organizations, like the markets they participate in, are in a constant state of flux.

> ...Strategy defines how all the elements of what a company does together. A strategy involves making choices throughout the value chain that are interdependent...Fit not only increases competitive advantage but also makes a strategy harder to imitate. Rivals can copy one activity or product feature fairly easily, but will have much more difficulty duplicating a whole system of competing.[3]

Consequently, the strategic value chain results management cycle is more dynamic, requires a multidimensional approach, needs continuous tracking of different situational factors, and must emphasize adaptation. It is here that the 4D Framework is more relevant. The four building blocks and parallel handling of those, plus a multidimensional approach create a new set of paradigms for the e-business transformations geared toward *continuity* of direction. It is this continuity that provides distinctiveness in the marketplace and reinforces any position the business is able to establish.

The application of the value chain technique brings together two sets of skills. The first skill has to do with the construction and documentation of a sound model, reflecting the situation that the organization wishes to address. The model provides indications of the targeted organizational states, the conditions and actions required to achieve these states, and the relationship of these targeted states to organizational success. This, in turn, leads to the creation of an overall value chain model. The more thought that goes into the construction of this model, the greater the chance of success.

The second skill involves the facilitation required to generate agreement on a particular situation. The development of the model and its analysis are powerful facilitative devices in and of themselves, enabling the organization to generate consensus around decisions and a com-

---

3. *Harvard Business Review*, May 2, 2000.

mitment to action. This creates a distinct value proposition that sets the organization apart from its competitors. This is vital in achieving any type of strategic positioning on the Internet.

An ongoing source of difficulty is that, in most instances, the immediate results of an investment will not represent the ultimate value chain results to the organization. The value chain program is the name given to the model resulting from the application of the value chain analysis and linkage to the 4D Framework elements.

The value chain program represents an effective way of integrating the e-investment cycle, defined as the delivery of the core investment's product and the value chain results cycle, which is defined as the delivery of the investment's expected results (see Figure 5–4). These enable the inducement of other results, leading eventually to an ultimate value chain model that is distinctive for the organization.

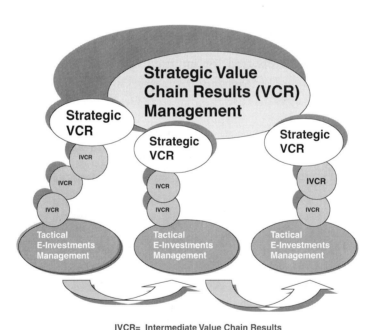

IVCR= Intermediate Value Chain Results

Figure 5–4   Linking the e-investment and value chain results management cycles through the value chain

▶ Value Chain Model Testing

Though subjective, the model created by the value chain program is amenable to detailed analysis. This process of analysis as it applies to the value chain model includes testing. Testing is an integral part of value chain analysis.

The process consists of testing the different entities of the value chain. The focus of validation may vary as a function of the situation at hand and of the particular phase of the value chain results cycle. Specifically, validation may focus on the following questions:

- How plausible are the relationships within the value chain?
- How achievable are the e-initiatives?

The testing process is designed to meet the specific requirements of the situation in terms of the strength of the value chain analysis required for key analysts to develop an appropriate level of confidence. The level of confidence in the model is a function of answers to testing questions and the quality of the information used to answer these questions. The information may be derived from processes involving replicated, observed, reported, or imputed results. It may be based on a small or large sample. It may draw on a number of sources, including individual judgments or opinions, secondary research (e.g., application of generic research and statistics to the situation), or primary research, which is carried out along the specific parameters of the situation.

All of the above factors will influence the quality and robustness of the input information used to validate different entities of the value chain. This, in turn, will influence the overall strength of value chain model, and ultimately its credibility with the key stakeholders.

E-Investment Bundles

The implementation of value chain results requires a broader view of the investment in terms of time, money, and technology. The implementation of designated value chain results corresponds to the realization of relevant value chain segments associated with the targeted four-dimensional value opportunities. This value accumulates until it defines the perceived goal, taking advantage of a marketable opportunity. The implementation of different results along a value chain segment often requires additional e-initiatives that were not part of the original analysis. These e-initiatives are a function of the specific constraints and conditions associated with the implementation of different results as the analysis progresses.

Each e-initiative can be seen as an investment, which is defined as a deliberate commitment of resources in view of achieving newly identified designated targets. Four-dimensional value opportunities generally involve multiple e-initiatives, including both core and ancillary investments of time, resources, and capital. Different four-dimensional value opportunities can be organized into four-dimensional value programs, which can be orchestrated around a core investment (e.g., a root e-initiative in a value chain model). In other words, a single investment in a core technology can fulfill several business "initiatives." Together, these ancillary investments, along with the core investment associated with a four-dimensional values program, form the e-investment bundles.

There may be cases where an e-investment bundle involves only the core investment. This would be an instance where the immediate results from the e-investment constitute the targeted value chain results and where no additional e-initiatives are required for achieving them.

▶ Putting It All Together

In accordance with the 4D Framework's principles, the impact of value chain results is best addressed within the context of a value chain program, as presented in Figure 5–5.

The value chain program involves four different phases, which are identical and in harmony with the phases of the 4D Framework:

Understanding Phase

- Value chain results identification

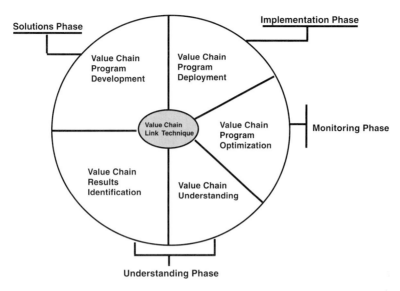

Figure 5–5   Value chain program

Value Chain Understanding Solutions Phase

- Value chain program development

Implementation Phase

- Value chain program deployment

Monitoring Phase

- Value chain program optimization

The value chain program addresses value chain entity identification and justification/testing. The change management, value chain results implementation, and tracking aspects are synonymous with the development and deployment phases. The optimization phase reinforces the dynamic nature of value chain results management, resulting from ongoing fine-tuning and tracking.

The value chain program is comprehensive and generic enough for the value chain program method to support the management of value chain results of past, current, and projected e-investments. It can be applied to a wide variety of e-investment situations (e.g., strategic, operational, and technological) at all levels of the organization. Within the 4D Framework, it complements the strategy, architecture, and change delivery methods.

▶ Phase 1: Understanding Phase

Value chain analysis, which is the main activity of this phase, has two components: opportunity recognition and justification.

Opportunity Recognition

The purpose of this component is to identify and qualify the different e-investment bundles and value chain results associated with a situation. This phase is designed to answer the following questions:

- What are the four-dimensional value opportunities associated with the situation?
- What are the e-investment bundles associated with the situation?
- What are the value chain results associated with a particular e-initiative?
- What is the nature and scope (e.g., organizational units involved) of the e-investment bundles associated with the situation?

The overall result of this component involves the identification of a *value proposition* for the organization. The value proposition describes the four-dimensional value opportunities as well as the nature and type of the individual e-initiatives associated with each of them. Together, these different e-initiatives represent the total e-investment or e-investment bundle associated with the value chain results opportunity.

A specific problem or opportunity may be related to any of these situations:

- The achievement of a specific e-business target, which represents a goal of the organization

- A particular e-investment, which represents a specific e-initiative under consideration, underway, or already completed by the organization
- An issue, which represents a problem or opportunity for key stakeholders that is not yet defined in terms of a particular target or e-investment

Justification

The purpose of this component is to evaluate and/or compare e-opportunities in terms of costs, risks, and potential value to the organization and to make appropriate recommendations.

The overall result of this phase involves a justification business case associated with a designated value proposition. The justification includes recommendations regarding an e-investment bundle and four-dimensional value opportunities as well as the side-effects associated with its implementation in a given organizational context.

A precondition of this phase is that a value proposition associated with a particular situation is available. It may be that a potential e-investment bundle has been identified from the opportunity recognition component. It may be that an e-investment has been identified independently by the organization or that it has been identified in the context of a strategy, architecture, or change delivery assignment.

This phase is designed to answer the following questions:

- What are the decision-making criteria and constraints associated with this particular e-investment bundle?
- What are the justification criteria and requirements associated with this particular e-investment bundle?
- What are the potential value chain results associated with this designated e-investment bundle?
- What is the most appropriate approach for testing the appropriateness and acceptability of this designated value proposition?
- What are the e-initiatives and observations that correspond to the implementation of the value chain results associated with this e-investment bundle?

- What are the required organizational changes to ensure that this e-investment bundle delivers targeted value chain results?
- What is the feasibility of the required organizational changes?
- What are the costs, risks, and value associated with this value chain results opportunity?

▶ Phase 2: Solutions Phase

The purpose of this phase is to develop a value chain link. A value chain link integrates all the e-initiatives required to materialize the designated value chain results and manage the organizational impacts and e-migration. It also addresses transition approaches, processes, resources, performance management requirements, and the infrastructure required to support the implementation-designated value chain results.

The overall result of this phase involves a value chain link. It is designed to answer the following questions:

- What is the best way to introduce the proposed changes in the organization (e-migration approach)?
- What are the additional e-initiatives required to manage the impacts on the organization and support the proposed e-migration approach?
- What infrastructure is required to support the deployment of the value chain link?
- What are the performance tracking and management requirements associated with the value chain link?
- What resources are required to support the implementation of the value chain link?
- What are the overall costs, risks, and value associated with the value chain link?

Preconditions for this phase are that an e-investment bundle or change e-initiative has been approved or is currently underway and that designated value chain results have been targeted for implementation.

▶ Phase 3: Implementation Phase

The purpose of this phase is to deploy a value chain link, ensure that emergent value chain results are identified, and that both planned and unplanned value chain results are achieved. Implementation was discussed in detail in Part 2 of this book as part of the discussion of the 4D Framework.

The overall result of this phase involves a deployed value chain program. This phase is designed to:

- Ensure that the appropriate value chain management processes are in place and working
- Ensure that the information required to assess the progress and results of the program on an ongoing basis is available
- Deal with unplanned value chain results as they emerge
- Review plans and projections as new information arises
- Recover planned and unplanned value chain results

A precondition for this phase is that a value chain link has been approved and is currently underway.

▶ Phase 4: Maintenance and Monitoring Phase

The purpose of this last phase of the value chain program is to fine-tune/adjust the value of past or ongoing e-investment e-initiatives. The overall result of this phase involves a value chain program monitoring plan.

This phase is specifically designed to:

- Ensure that ongoing or past projects are yielding all potential value chain results
- Extend the useful life of an ongoing value chain link
- Leverage different assets and states resulting from current or past e-investments

▶ The Value Chain Linking Technique

Concepts and Principles

The value chain is based on the notion that one's line of reasoning can provide a basis for relating and positioning a range of value chain results relative to e-investments and for understanding the implementation of these results. There is always logic that could be made explicit relative to how results could be related and obtained from an e-investment. Peoples' thoughts, arguments, and intuition can be mapped and structured into a cohesive set of mapping components to support problem analysis and decision-making and account for benefit evaluation and implementation.

The Basic Link Map

The basic link map corresponds to the skeleton of the value chain. It is the basic structure of reasoning whereby results are associated to one or many specific e-investments. It constitutes a valid way of understanding how certain results can be induced from particular e-investments. It provides a basis for appreciating how certain results can be materialized based on particular e-investments.

The following example illustrates the basic reasoning involved in the decision to implement an e-ERM system.

The content and structure of the line of reasoning illustrated in the example can be described in a basic link map. A basic link map is formed from two types of components: value chain results (final and immediate) and e-initiatives. Figure 5–6 illustrates the basic link map for the example.

At the root of the logic, the e-investment, which represents an e-initiative, affects two different types of results: final and immediate. Each of these first-order results can in turn contribute to other value chain results or enable the execution of other e-initiatives. Ultimately,

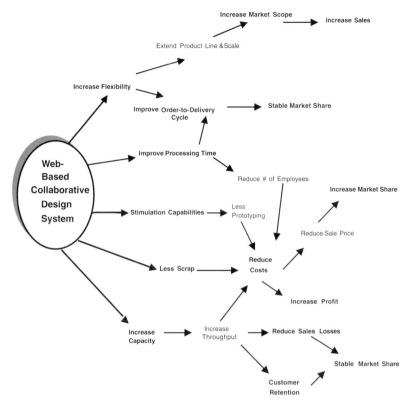

Figure 5–6 Illustration of the basic map associated with an e-collaboration system's implementation

these logically linked elements form paths; these logical paths then form a basic link map.

Additional E-Initiatives

An additional e-initiative is a mapping entity that refers to an action that is considered necessary, in addition to an already identified e-initiative.

In the previous example, some additional e-initiatives can be added to the basic link map insofar as they are considered conditions necessary to the achievement of designated results. Indeed, while considering the e-investment in an collaborative design system, managers were also aware that these systems would not deliver all of their potential value chain results without some additional changes to the organization. They were aware that the effective use of these systems would require training, a change in plant layout, along with a change in employee responsibilities and a new reward system. Figure 5–7 shows how these additional e-initiatives can be added to the basic link map and related to the relevant results.

In this figure, another e-initiative has been added to the basic link map and related to the results (final and immediate): improved order-to-delivery cycle. Indeed, the achievement of increased flexibility and improved processing time were not considered sufficient in and of themselves to induce an improvement in the order-to-delivery cycle. A change in shipping procedures was also considered necessary to achieve an improved order-to-delivery cycle.

It is possible to distinguish the following types of results:

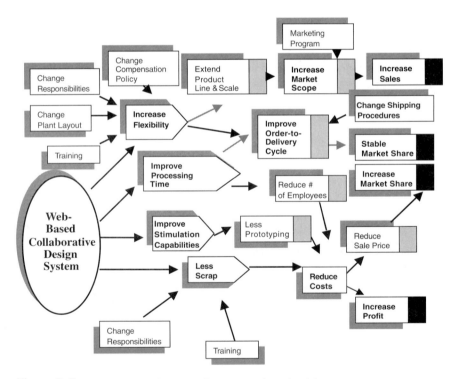

Figure 5–7   Basic line of reasoning associated with an e-collaborative design system

Chapter **5** | Value Chain Analysis

- **Immediate value chain results**—An immediate result is directly related to a root e-initiative. In the example, the initial investment is associated with six first-order results (immediate): increased flexibility, improved processing time, improved simulation capabilities, less scrap, reduced rework, and increased capacity.

- **Final results**—Final results consist of the last results of a link map. The final results of the basic link map, as they are formulated in the collaborative design example, are: increased sales, stable market share, increased market share, and increased profit.(See Figure 5–8.)

E-Initiatives

E-initiatives are components of the basic link map that refer to actions that can contribute to the achievement of any results (immediate and final). Initiatives always refer to an element that can be acted on directly. Number of employees, plant layout, and work procedures are examples of elements whose state can be changed or influenced by acting on them directly.

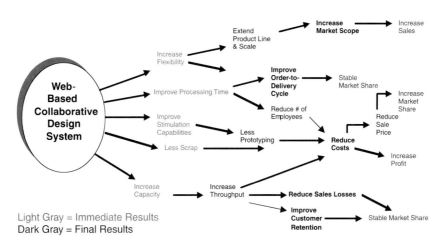

Figure 5–8   E-initiatives

When they are part of a basic link map, e-initiatives are called path e-initiatives. The basic difference between the notion of a result (immediate and final) and an e-initiative resides in the notion of direct versus indirect access.

▶ Value Chain Notation and Rules

A value chain model is composed of four basic modeling components: results (immediate and final), e-initiatives, and the value chain matrix.

Results

Within a value chain model, results (immediate and final) are represented as two rectangles: one with a shaded stopper (final) and the other with a non-shaded stopper (see Figure 5–9).

Any result (immediate or final) bears a label that refers to a change or maintenance in the state of an object. This label is formulated in terms of the result. It is usually formulated in terms of a noun or a word group preceded by a qualifier (e.g., increased customer service, stable level of quality).

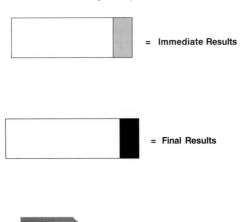

= Immediate Results

= Final Results

= E-Initiatives

Figure 5–9   Value chain models represent results (immediate and final)

Any result (immediate or final) can be duplicated within a value chain model. In this instance, it keeps the same identifier and label.

E-Initiatives (Business, People, Process, and Technology)

Within a value chain model, e-initiatives are represented as rectangles with one pointed end. Each e-initiative has an identifier (number).

An e-initiative bears a label that is formulated in terms of an action (imperative form).

Value Chain Matrix

In this matrix, all other entities, results, e-initiatives, and influencers are categorized into different slots as shown in Figure 5–10. So if we have business results, we put them under business and goals; if there are process goals, we put them under process and ultimate goals, and so on. The rows are fixed, but the columns depend on the context of the e-business project.

Sometimes, if the value chain analysis becomes too complex, there can be just one column and we may focus on only one or two rows (see Figure 5–10).

Combining and differentiating results (immediate and final) from e-initiatives is a two-step process:

Step 1—In value chain analysis, we do not always strictly differentiate between results and e-initiatives. What we do is identify the e-initiatives and results and represent them as ovals and place them in the value chain matrix. In fact, all the entities are represented as ovals.

This is needed to keep things simple—collect the appropriate entities and keep them in the right slots. However, in the later stage of the value chain program, that is, in the value chain linking stage, the results and e-initiatives need to be separated. At a conceptual level, this

	Finances	Products	Markets	Goals
Business				
People				
Process				
Technology				

Figure 5–10   Value chain matrix analysis

seems to be a trivial job; at a detailed level, the two can be very confusing. An example of an oval is shown below:

Market
Share

Step 2—The purpose of this step is to explain how to identify, from the set of already formulated components, the components that should be modeled as e-initiatives and to represent them as such in the basic link map.

As mentioned previously, new components added to a basic link map are modeled as ovals. However, as the basic link map takes shape, e-initiatives should be differentiated from results (immediate and final) because they are defined in terms of an object that can or cannot be acted on directly in the specified organizational context. This differentiation also applies to components modeled as e-initiatives, which are in fact results (immediate and final). As the basic link map evolves, it may be necessary to transform components that were initially thought of as e-initiatives into results. In this case, it may also be necessary to identify true e-initiatives connected with these new results.

6

Value Chain Program and Value Chain Linking

▶ Value Chain Linking

Value chain linking, as discussed in the previous chapter, links the ultimate goals of an organization with its e-initiatives. It connects e-initiatives with some immediate results and ultimately the final result in a series of chain links. Value chain linkage techniques also assess how much each e-initiative may affect the immediate and final results. This is measured via an "e-effectiveness quotient," which is expressed in fractions or percentages. The e-effectiveness quotient, is a critical item that discusses the viability and importance of an e-initiative in relationship to the goals to be achieved. Too often, e-initiatives are undertaken because they are thought to be "good ideas," without analyzing their effect on the final organizational goals. This leads to unsuccessful projects or projects that may be implemented successfully, but the business value realized is sub-optimal.

With the advent of so many dot-com "busts," it is crucial that all e-initiatives are justified in terms of their effectiveness and not just their efficiency. It is also important that all e-initiatives are aligned and harmonious and do not create a negative impact as a whole. Two perfectly fine e-business projects may be cannibalizing other e-initiatives when judged in the context of organizational goals. This becomes even more important when e-business initiatives are cross-enterprise.

Value chain development helps managers and professionals manage the value chain results from an e-investment. Prior to presenting some of the preferred approaches and solutions, this chapter will outline the inherent challenges as well as the basic concepts associated with the identification, evaluation, and implementation of value chain results.

The in-depth analysis of numerous e-initiatives as well as the unpredictability of results associated with large-scale organizational change point to the difficulties of bringing about lasting improvements in organizations. One of the inherent difficulties with value chain results identification is that value chain results are dynamic. They are a function of perception and context. An e-initiative can produce a range of results that can potentially represent desired value chain results depending on the way they are perceived, but because markets and business are dynamic, it is how these results are viewed over time that is critical.

▶ The Value Chain: A Detailed Link Map

A value chain consists of a basic link map along with a set of peripheral conditions that represent conditions for the implementation of desired results. The peripheral conditions, which represent additional sources of contribution, include observations and additional e-initiatives. A value chain link therefore consists of a detailed link map as defined in the previous chapter.

Once completed, a value chain includes a basic link map along with a set of peripheral conditions referring to relevant additional sources of contribution, be they actionable elements (additional e-initiatives), uncontrolled elements, or *a priori* elements (observations). It usually forms a detailed network through which each result can be positioned relative to specific e-investments and to the other components involved in its implementation. It can elucidate and handle many of the hidden aspects of value chain results implementation.

Principles of Multiple Cause-Effect

Cause-effect relationships involve situations where one element is said to be the cause of another, that is, the first element is viewed as both necessary and sufficient to induce the other. Hence, the resulting element is defined by the causing entity.

However, many-to-one cause-effect relationships are quite different from one-to-one cause-effect relationships. Because a cause is, of course, necessary but not always solely sufficient for the effect to be realized, it may not provide a complete explanation for the occurrence of the product. There can always be other necessary conditions and causes that can be identified in connection with a specific effect or result.

The building of a value chain requires a clear distinction between these two kinds of relationships. In a value chain, each time a relation is made between two entities of a basic link map, this relationship is thought of as many-to-one relationship. Thus, at the onset, each path relationship within the map conveys a partial, rather than a full determination of, the resulting entity. This principle implies that there may sometimes be additional (necessary) sources of causes for a result to be realized.

Rules for Value Chain Linkage

These rules refer to the way different entities can be related. This section provides rules as to how the relationships between different entities should be created.

Value Chain Results Rule

A result (immediate) is always linked to another result (final and immediate) or e-initiative (Figure 6–1).

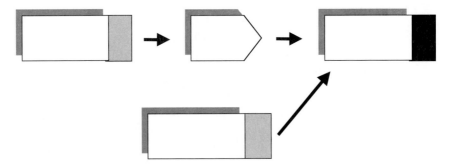

Figure 6–1   Results (final and immediate) configuration rules

Value Chain Transformation

In Figure 6–2, we see that a value chain analysis entity, represented by an oval, can be a value chain result or an e-initiative. So, the first step is to create a simple chain.

In Figure 6–3, the ovals are changed into value chain results and e-initiatives.

Integrity Rules

For a link map to be consistent, it should satisfy the following rules:

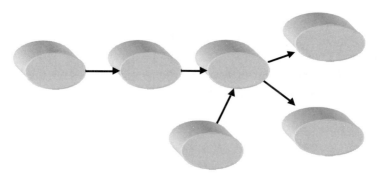

Figure 6–2   Value chain analysis

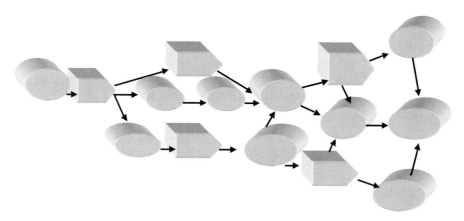

Figure 6–3 A possible configuration of value chain entities

Distinction Rule

- The distinction rule is used to ensure that value chain results are clearly differentiated from e-initiatives. E-initiatives that can be carried out through proactive organizational actions need to be clearly differentiated in the map.

- By definition, a result exists in the state of an element that can no longer be acted on directly. Mapping part of a link map as a result means that it refers to (or has as its object) an element that cannot be acted on directly. By definition, an e-initiative consists of an action, thus it refers to an element that can be acted on directly. Mapping parts of a link map as e-initiatives means that they can be acted on directly.

- Figure 6–4 illustrates the case where the application of the distinction rule led to changes in a map's entities. The *reduced # of features* in a product refers to something that can be acted on directly. Thus, it can be changed to an e-initiative.

It is important to note that discriminating between what should be mapped as a value chain result rather than as an e-initiative is not always an easy task. There are situations where a specific element could be mapped either as a result or as an e-initiative. Thus, differentiation between results and e-initiatives in a map link requires judgment.

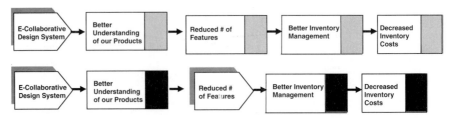

Figure 6–4   Application of the distinction rule

E-Effectiveness Quotient and Rule

The effect of an e-initiative on a value chain result or another e-initiative is measured in terms of what is called the "e-effectiveness quotient." This is a number from 0 to 1. 0 means the effect is minimal and hence is an e-initiative that needs to be eliminated; 1 indicates a very strong e-initiative. In a link map where several e-initiatives may affect a value chain result, the effectiveness quotient will highlight the importance of each e-initiative in achieving the targeted value chain result.

Other Rules

Entities of a basic link map cannot be indirectly related to themselves. More specifically, there should be no direct bidirectional relationships between two entities of the map, nor should there be any circularity or "loop" between the different paths or segments of the map. A link map that involves a one-time implementation is not designed to study recurrent phenomena.

Within a value chain link, path segments cannot be materialized in exactly the same way and according to the same additional conditions more than once. According to an underlying value chain principle, two successive passes in a logical sequence would involve different additional e-initiatives and observations as organizational states evolve through time. A value chain program would therefore not materialize exactly the same way at different points in time. Each repetitive implementation would have to be considered as a function of new conditions, dictated by a different context.

Value Chain Formulation Modes

Value chain formulation involves the development of complete logic or a line of reasoning whereby specific results can be obtained from a set of e-initiatives. Formulation modes consist of the way in which different entities of the map are elicited and added to the map from the standpoint of entities of a value chain in development.

Left-to-Right Mode

The left-to-right mode consists of extending a value chain by adding entities that logically follow one another (see Figure 6–5). The forward mode helps the analyst identify the different impacts or states that can be generated from a given e-initiative or organizational state. It tends to focus on the potential impacts and consequences of a particular element in the map. In a left-to-right mode, logical impacts and consequences of an entity are elicited and added to the map.

It is important to justify where a value chain is developed from the e-investment point of view. In this case, the e-investment represents the focus of attention from which a link map can be developed in terms of potential impacts and value chain results.

Right-to-Left Mode

The right-to-left mode consists of extending a value chain by adding entities that logically precede another component from which the reasoning is anchored, be it from a formulation starting point or another entity that has already been formulated (see Figure 6–6). The right-to-left mode helps identify the different means and requirements for achieving a targeted state. It tends to focus on how a targeted state can be achieved. In this backward mode, things that can contribute to an entity are elicited and added to the map.

The right-to-left mode will rarely constitute the only way through which a complete value chain can be built. It is important in strategic projects to replace the usual top-down approach. In this case, these targets represent the focus of attention from which a link map can be developed regarding states as well as e-initiatives from which these targets could be achieved.

Inside-Out Mode

As suggested by the name, the inside-out mode consists of a combination of the two preceding modes (see Figure 6–7). In fact, it does not represent a pure or basic formulation mode. It corresponds to a situation where the value chain formulation requires an extensive use of the two basic modes. This situation requires the right-to-left mode to identify relevant root e-initiatives or options to solve problems as well as the left-to-right mode to identify desirable states that could be associated with these issues.

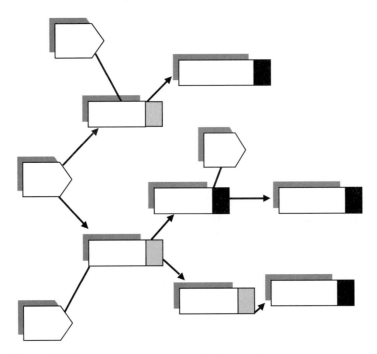

Figure 6–5   Left-to-right value chain mode

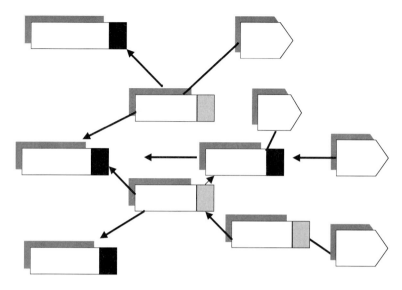

Figure 6–6　Right-to-left value chain mode

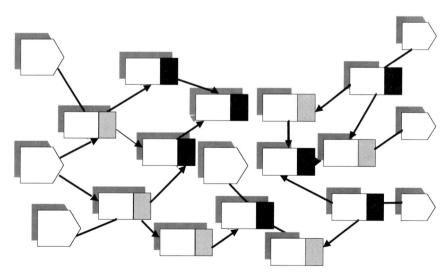

Figure 6–7　Inside-out value chain mode

The Value Chain Link Process Summarized

The value chain linkage can be summarized by a basic set of steps and guidelines involved in developing a link map. This section describes these basic steps and provides some guidelines to facilitate the formulation process. It involves five different phases, which were discussed in detail in Chapter 4.

1. **Understanding (initial) phase**—The purpose of this step is to gather sufficient information to determine the appropriate starting point. This often starts with the value chain matrix of entities provided by a value chain analysis. A requisite level of information has to be generated about the problem or situation at hand before beginning the construction of a value chain. This information may be available, enabling the value chain formulation starting points to be readily identified. Often, the situation from which the value chain should be built requires that a preliminary investigation be carried out for the key problems, objectives, and other relevant issues to be elicited and mapped into relevant formulation starting points.

   This step can usually be realized through interviews with relevant individuals.

2. **Understanding phase (Where do we start?)**—A starting point corresponds to an object of interest from which a value chain link can be formulated. It consists of the value chain analysis entities (ovals) from which a basic link map can be developed. In some circumstances, the starting point is easy to identify. Part of the situation to be investigated may be already defined or understood in such a way for the first mapping entities to be formulated. In other cases, some preliminary fact-finding may be required to determine the appropriate formulation starting points.

   There are essentially three different types of mapping starting points. The first one concerns the case where an e-investment has to be justified (e.g., the introductory point of a CRM system). In other instances, the mapping starting point is a defined target within the organization (e.g., reduce costs by X%; reduce the product development cycle by X%; improve customer satisfaction). In these cases, targeted results are already established and represent the targeted results within the value chain link.

The job here is to determine how different e-initiatives and results can be effectively linked to the targeted results (final and immediate). Most e-businesses or transformed e-businesses fall into this category. The final case represents an instance where no particular e-investment or preferred target has been identified in advance. This is the case where a value chain link is developed from the issues of the situation. These may equally stem from bottom-up changes required for the current situation as from broader top-down business problems.

3. **Solutions phase (initial value chain link map)**—The purpose of this step is to generate all the different lines of reasoning emanating from and/or leading to the formulation starting points, forming a preliminary basic link map. The goal during this step is to generate as many map entities as possible from the formulation starting point(s) in an unconstrained way relative to map composition and configuration rules, preciseness, completeness, and validity (Figure 6–8).

    Generating a preliminary basic logic is not unlike a brainstorming exercise. It consists of representing, without hesitation, more or less integrated entities of one's line of reasoning. To encourage the fluidity of this generative process, all of the reasoning's entities are mapped as value chain results, whatever their actual status. The ultimate result of this step is a preliminary map that will be clarified and extended in the future.

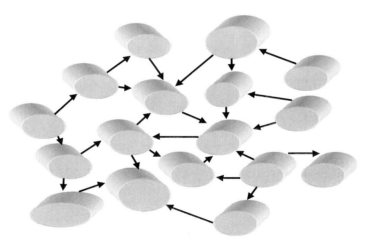

Figure 6–8   Development of a basic value chain link map

4. **Solutions phase (distinguish value chain results from e-initiatives)**—The purpose of this step is to identify the e-initiatives and represent them in the basic link map.

   As mentioned previously, new entities added to a basic link map are mapped as results notwithstanding their effective nature. This lack of preciseness and attention to rules is proposed to facilitate the formulation process. However, as the basic link map takes shape, e-initiatives should be differentiated from results (e.g., differentiation rule) on the basis that they are defined in terms of an entity that can or cannot be acted on directly in the specified organizational context.

   The distinction rule also applies to entities mapped as e-initiatives that are in fact value chain results. As the basic link map evolves, it may also be necessary to transform entities that were considered e-initiatives into value chain results.

5. **Maintenance (fine-tuning and support)**—Once a basic link map has been developed through the application of rules and preceding activities, another important step involves the identification of additional, necessary conditions for the realization of the basic link map. In this step, additional sources of contribution regarding the implementation of some of the entities of the basic link map are recognized.

   To execute this step, one considers the incoming links (effects) to an entity and questions whether other elements, in addition to those involved in the incoming link(s), are required for the implementation of the designated entities (e.g., value chain results).

Important Guidelines

Here are some guidelines that should be applied along with the mapping process:

Use the Organization's Language

The value chain link should as much as possible reflect the organization's language. The language of the organization can be defined as the specialized vocabulary used in the organization as well as throughout its industry. It is also the language that reflects individual organizational and industry-related idiosyncrasies.

This constitutes an important guideline to the extent that it is important for the map to predominantly reflect the user's input. To foster a sense of ownership, the user should recognize and appreciate his or her contribution to the map and really understand it. Finally, using the organization's language in the map facilitates understanding of the map, its communication effectiveness, as well as its acceptance by key stakeholders.

Use Proactive Value Chain Link Language

The value chain link elements should be formulated in terms of proactive actions and results as opposed to problems and deficiencies. For example, somebody may say that the company has problems managing its inventory information: "The information about our finances is not precise enough," or "Information about ROI is rarely up-to-date." In a value chain link, this information should be represented as follows: *more precise financial information* and *up-to-date financial information*.

▶ Summary

The various stages of value chain linking steps (as summarized in Figure 6–9) have been discussed in this chapter. The point is to not just create a valid operations map, but to make it manageable. If the problem and organizational culture demand it, value chain links can be simplified or made more complex depending on the need.

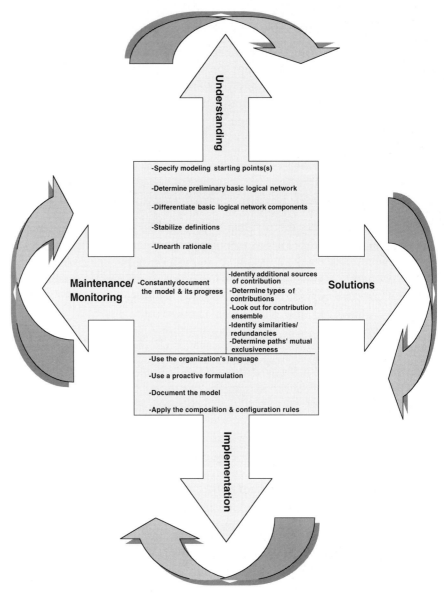

Figure 6–9   Value chain process and guidelines

Part 4

Where to Now?

Velocity of the value-adding process. Competitors with the shortest product development, manufacturing and distribution cycles usually dominate their markets because they have the advantage of innovation, flexibility, responsiveness, and low cost.

Velocity of the change process. To thrive today, an organization must be able to transform itself and its underlying business strategy quickly and efficiently if it is to fend off fast evolving threats and make the most of fleeting opportunities.[1]

Now that we have explored the tools to assess and design turnaround e-solutions, we need the means to implement them. We need tools to put our grand design into effect within and/or across any organization that wants to meet the grueling requirements of developing and maintaining a successful e-business. The rest of this book will explore two of the most important tools in the 4D Framework: high-velocity process management (HVPM) to put into action the high-level process transformations defined by our value chain analysis, and a strategic change management system to deal with both ongoing implementation and long-term maintenance once our e-initiatives are firmly in place.

HVPM is one of the foundations of the 4D Framework. It takes the elements, tools, and concepts from all the previous process redesign disciplines and adds effective multitasking and parallelism to collapse the cycle times to redesign business processes. The 4D Framework as applied to an e-business requires business processes to be redesigned and deployed rapidly. The trick to doing this is to choose the right high-impact business processes (or sub-processes) and apply highly skilled process experts to look at different aspects of the process, namely workflow, technologies, organizational culture, the business and financial impacts of change, change management, and so on. This holistic, iterative approach makes the fuzzy mass of high-velocity processes move rapidly from an "as-is" stage to a "to-be" stage.

Change management in e-business represents an essential component of e-business transformation. It is often neglected or its value realized too late in the game. In this book, change management in e-business principles is incorporated in the 4D Framework. It complements other aspects of the 4D Framework by providing the concepts, processes, and techniques designed specifically to support the implementation of large-scale organizational change toward e-business transformation.

1. http://www.highvelocity.com/velocity.asp

High-Velocity Process Management

▶ High-Velocity Process Management (HVPM) Revisited

HVPM describes the concepts, activities, and deliverables associated with analyzing, designing, and implementing e-business processes for an organization. The method is based on the 4D Framework. In this chapter, we will generalize and summarize the whole methodology and explain the important features that are essential in e-business process transformations.

The intent of this section is to provide a practical method to help e-business designers either redesign existing business processes or design completely new business processes.

Before delving into the "high-velocity" part, some basic process concepts and techniques need to be discussed.

How to Create "High Velocity"

Table 7–1 shows how to develop a new process. Each of the six top-level events is called a "phase." The events that are part of each phase are called "activities." The actual assessment and design activities, the heart of the method, are described as tasks and procedures.

Table 7–1   Overall High-Velocity Process Management

		Activities	Tasks and Procedures
Understanding Phase	New Process Request Reviewed	• New Process Request Initiated • New Process Request Qualified	
	Current Situation Assessed	• Assessment Team Built • Assessment Technique Chosen • Assessment Plan Made	• Assessment Executed • Assessment Reviewed
Solutions Phase	New Process Designed	• Process Design Team Built • Process Design Work Planned • Process Design Work Executed	
	New Process Validated	• Process Validation Team Selected • Validation Criteria Selected • Validation Executed	
	New Process Approved	• New Process Design Presented • New Process Design Approved	

Table 7–1   Overall High-Velocity Process Management (Continued)

		Activities	Tasks and Procedures
Implementation Phase	New Process Implemented	• Pilot Process Implemented • New Process Fully Implemented • Continuous Improvement Program Implemented	

For each phase of the method, this chapter includes a phase diagram showing the main activities and participants. Each activity is described by:

- The objective of the activity
- The requirements
- Specific roles and responsibilities
- Dependencies

Roles and Responsibilities

The project office (PO) is responsible for the planning and control of the development of new business processes and ensuring that the process assessment and design reports are presented to the testing and approval teams.

The qualification team is responsible for:

- Reviewing the request for a new or redesigned process
- Deciding if a process assessment or design activity should take place

The understanding team is responsible for assessing the current business process. It is responsible for planning the understanding phase, developing the new process design in accordance with the design plan, and producing a new process design report in accordance with the standard new process design format.

The solutions team is responsible for planning the new process design, executing the new design process, and producing a new process design report in accordance with the standard new process design format.

The validation team is responsible for:

- Validating the accuracy and fairness of the new process assessment report
- Assessing the reasonableness and practicality of the new process design set out in the new process design report

The approval team is responsible for reviewing the new process design in accordance with the new process design criteria and:

- Accepting the new design without amendment
- Accepting the new design with amendment(s)
- Rejecting the new design

The process design expert (recommended profile: management consultant) is responsible for:

- Ensuring that the process models are drawn in accordance with 4D Framework conventions
- Providing advice on the design of process performance measures
- Facilitating workshops when requested by the process team leader
- Integrating the overall process architecture

The process team leader (recommended profile: management consultant) is responsible for:

- Organizing workshops
- Preparing all materials for the team
- Facilitating the workshops
- Preparing assessment and design reports

Teams are made up of representatives of different organizations and business units, plus independent management consultants (see Table 7–2).

Table 7–2 Template for BPR

	BPR Team	Team Member(s)
Understanding Phase	Qualification Team	• User Representative • Customer Representative • Process Design Experts
Understanding Phase	Assessment Team	• Client Representative • Process Design Expert • User Process Representative • Process Owner • Project Control Office • Core Process Team Leader
Solutions Phase	Design Team	• Client Representative • Process Design Expert • User Process Representative • Process Owner • Project Control Office • Core Process Team
Solutions Phase	Validation Team	• User Representative • Customer Representative • Process Owner
Solutions Phase	Approval Team	• Executive Customer Representatives • Core Process Team Leader • Project Control Office
Implementation Phase	Transition Management Team	• Transition Manager • Core Process Team Leader

The steering committee is responsible for:

- Seeing that the project is in line with the organizational objectives
- Change is brought in at a high level
- Project is on-schedule and on-budget

There are also sub-teams according to specialty: business teams, people teams, process teams, and technology teams.

The *mobile team* is the most critical team in creating the speed that is needed. The mobile team consists of four senior people from four backgrounds: business/people/process/technology. Their job is to interface with different sub-teams at different phases and keep communicating the main deliverables and concepts.

The new design team should be composed of the same people as the understanding team as they will have experienced the workshops and understand the context for the new design. They will have come together as a team by this stage and will be used to working together. When there are several different processes being assessed and redesigned simultaneously, some participants may be part of two or more different process teams. Therefore, it is important that each process team leader follows the same phases, activities, and procedures, and uses the same presentation graphics so that the method that is being applied is consistent for each.

Summary

The HVPM phase and techniques are summarized in Table 7–3. The holistic approach, combined with the phases and execution in parallel, make this approach effective and efficient. The 4D Framework allows the handling of both types of process changes. HVPM also insists on starting from the results desired, which is known as right-to-left thinking. This allows the e-initiatives and process redesigns to stay aligned with the goals desired. This also speeds up process redesign and implementation. However, the 4D Framework maintains that under certain conditions, inside-out thinking or left-to-right thinking may be more appropriate. This was discussed in the previous chapter. Other basic principles embedded in HVPM are shown in Figure 7–1.

The principles shown in Figure 7–1 are self-explanatory and have been discussed in previous chapters of this book.

HVPM will help companies that are embarking on simple e-commerce projects; however, the biggest impact of HVPM will be on large e-business and transformed e-business-type initiatives. It is very clear from earlier discussions that in the e-business world:

- Customers are taking control.
- Competition has intensified extremely.
- Change is constant.

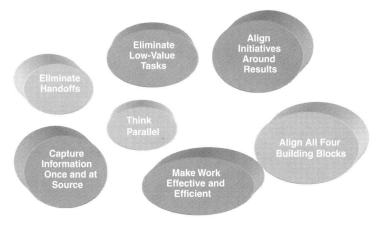

Figure 7–1 Basic principles in HVPM

Hammer and Champy state in their famous book, *Reengineering the Corporation*,[1] that some of the possible solutions are:

- Combine several jobs into one.
- Allow workers to make decisions.
- Perform steps in a process in a natural order.
- Perform work where it makes the most sense.

In a digital world, all these solutions have taken an elevated stature. E-competition is especially intense, customers are really taking control, and change is mind-boggling. The 4D Framework and HVPM, while taking the best practices and disciplines from the "Old Economy," have also taken into account the speed effect.

The speed and ensuing quality demanded in a digital world can only be reached with a holistic combination of proper processes, enabling technologies, and work culture changes. The productivity increases demanded can no longer be achieved by just reducing work and handoffs; enabling technology needs to replace them.

1. Hammer, Michael, and James Champy, *Reengineering the Corporation* (New York: HarperBusiness, A Division of HarperCollinsPublishers, 1993).

Table 7-3   High-Velocity Process Management

Project Components

Project Phases		Customer	Problems, Opportunities, Benefits, and Costs	Processes	Technology	People	Culture	Organization
Understanding Phase	Initiation		Determine Scope					Communication Plan
	Current Analysis	Interview	Identify Opportunities	Model As-Is and Measure	Understand	Interview	Assess	Understand
Solutions Phase	Re-engineering	Test Ideas		Model and Simulate To-Be	Identify Enablers	Re-engineering Workshops	Identify Supporting Changes Needed	Vision, Goals, Objectives, Principles
	Transition		Priorities, Quick Hits, Benefits, Costs	Transition Steps	Identify System Requirements	Workshops	Changes to Jobs, Communication, Procedures	Redesign
Implementation Phase	Implementation	Communication Plan	Implementation Strategy and Plan			Hiring/Training	Change Management Plan	Communication Plan

HVPM has been developed in two distinct steps. We have first applied the 4D Framework phases and chosen the tasks and methodologies that are needed to do e-business process redesigns. Once the "whats" have been defined, the tasks should be organized in such a parallel way that HVPM becomes the appropriate answer for the digital needs, namely speed and high velocity. The 4D phases apply very well with HVPM in the following paragraphs. The tasks and deliverables are typically described at a high level and a hypothetical case study (based on real situation) with some real life examples have been given in the next few sections.

▶ Understanding Phase

In this phase, the following tasks need to be performed:

Conduct current analysis:

- Identify processes that need to be redesigned in an e-business context. (See Figure 7–2.)
- Estimate the depth of change.
- Analyze the current business processes.
- Compare with "best practices" and build a matrix of key measurables.
- Analyze the organizational culture and adoption to change styles.

Develop future vision:

- Develop a redesigned process vision (high-level).
- Establish a performance matrix for key process measurables.
- Develop a change vision.

In all of the team building activities mentioned earlier, one of the important things that a team can establish is a list of team rules. This is absolutely a critical success factor for e-teams, which work in parallel to establish teaming norms uniformly throughout sub-teams. This

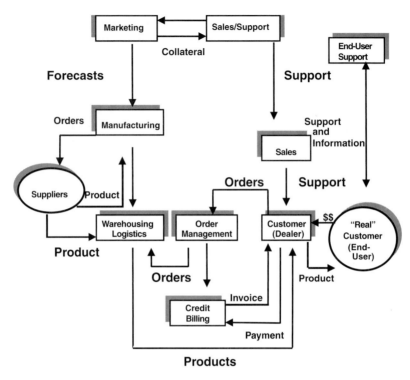

Figure 7–2 Example of initial scope determination

reduces the team conflicts and inefficiencies that are so important in recreating processes in a high-velocity manner. Example rules include:

- All information will be available to all team members.
- No idea is stupid.
- Challenge the foundation—practice out-of-the-box thinking.
- Encourage internal freedom to say anything.
- All members must participate.
- All members should report to the program manager (even if they have been transferred from individual departments for the duration of the project).
- All members should respond to each other promptly, courteously, and with no personal attacks.
- The program manager will continuously encourage feedback from the team.

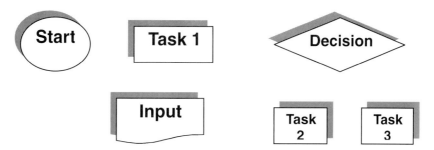

Figure 7–3   Example of a flowchart

Other activities like team alignment are evident from Figure 7–3. Teams can be formed to deal with analyzing and visioning the business issues, process issues, cultural issues, change issues, and technology issues depicted in the diagram. The ultimate result should be the creation of a high-level, new vision for the business, people, process, and technology aspects of a process.

Next, brainstorming sessions of several parallel teams can decide which tasks need refinement, which need elimination, etc. Based on this discussion, a current process flow, as drawn in Figure 7–4, will emerge. Note that the figure could use four different color schemes for the four different strategies of each work step or task in the process flow.

Let's look at the possible results of a hypothetical study:

Huge amounts of data were collected for each work step. A performance matrix (see Figure 7–5) was created, which included statistics for how much labor was needed for a certain task (also known as a full-time equivalent, or FTE) and the cycle time for each work step.

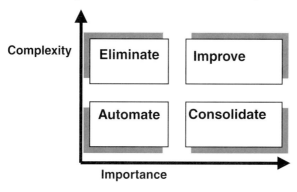

Figure 7–4   Task effectiveness quadrant

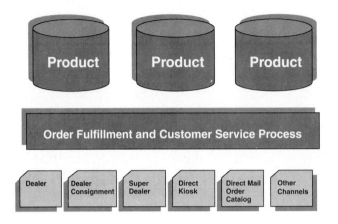

Vision Will Be Flexible to End-User Demands for New Products or Convenient Channels

Product   Product   Product

Order Fulfillment and Customer Service Process

| Dealer | Dealer Consignment | Super Dealer | Direct Kiosk | Direct Mail Order Catalog | Other Channels |

Benefits:
- Multiple channels meet customer needs and support growth goals.
- Channel management is critical to profitability.
- Information will be gathered through all channels.
- Dealer agreement will be drastically changed.
- Shift in marketing focus--demand generation will be driven.
- System will leverage economies of scale.

Figure 7–5   End-user demands on new products/channel

This data was collected from computer systems, from interviews, and from checking paper records. These statistics were compared with industry best practices. When the new process was designed, the matrix gave solid efficiency numbers for the digital process.

Typical Deliverables

The organization produced several deliverables at the understanding stage. Some important deliverables (with examples) are:

1. **Vision statement of the channels)**—The team found out through structured interviews and analyses of best practices that its dealer-only channels needed to be replaced with all channels, including the Internet, for the following reasons:

- Customers demanded quicker turnaround, higher QoS, and fewer delivery errors.
- Employees needed to be thoroughly retrained to handle the huge volumes and quality services demanded.
- As a result, the performance matrix needed to be redesigned to align employees' compensation and skill development with key business objectives.

So a clearly stated vision statement on the identified domain is a very important deliverable.

2. **New business process design (high-level)**—Unnecessary tasks were eliminated, handoffs reduced, and the new order processing business process had a much reduced cycle time. The number of FTEs was also reduced. At a high level, the new process looked like Figure 7–6.

3. **Cost savings analysis (high-level)**—Here, the team determined the annual cost of non-Web order fulfillment and customer service processes and then determined the annual cost of the new

The New Business Model Emphasizes Profitability and Flexibility to Customer Needs

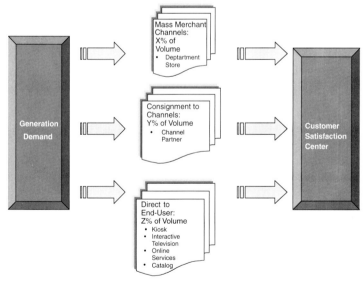

Figure 7–6 Business model emphasizes profitability and flexibility to customer needs

Web-enabled order fulfillment and order entry processes (see Figure 7–7). There was an annual cost reduction of 30%. This cost reduction was due to the reduction of FTEs, interest payment on money used to hold inventories (effect of less inventory), and payment on mainframe technology. The team showed that the end-to-end cycle time would be reduced by 35%. That alone increased efficiencies and affected the bottom line directly. The operating costs of missed business for not going to the Internet and not changing the business processes were calculated to be almost 45% of the current revenue of the organization. These values were then benchmarked against industry standards and justified.

At the end of the understanding phase, the team had to make a decision to go/no go. In this case, the decision was to go to the next phase.

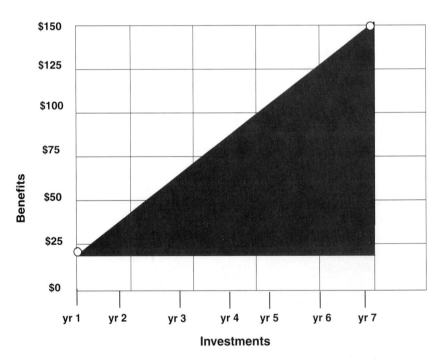

Figure 7–7   Executive summary total benefits and investments

▶ Solutions Phase

The solutions phase undertaken by an organization consists of the following activities.

Develop new processes:

- Eliminate (further) unnecessary work steps and create effective workflows and information flows.
- Use, as needed, value chain methods to uncover the proper e-initiatives and change management initiatives and link them with the business/people/process/technology goals.
- Establish Web technologies by selecting the right vendors, choosing the proper methodologies, and choosing the right consulting companies.

Develop business case:

- Develop a detailed cost/benefit analysis for the high-velocity process redesign.
- Assess the impact of change in-depth.
- Assess training/education/communication costs and benefits.

Plan implementation:

- Create an implementation plan to test out the new organization as a whole via an "organizational prototype," which is a testing method that tests a small version of the new business process using the new technologies, a subset of customers, and all the redesigned work procedures.
- Plan a high-level change management program.

The team should use the redesign that was started in the understanding phase as a baseline and go much deeper. Using HVPM techniques, the e-team may be broken up into two major groups: one looking at one set of sub-processes and the other at other sub-processes. Each of these groups may be further subdivided to work in parallel.

The program manager coordinates the small team activities and feeds information from one group to another in a consistent and summarized fashion. Every week, all sub-group leads should meet to do cross-team brainstorming. This can enhance the speed of the redesign effort.

Small and expanded teams may also take part in vendor and technology selection. Also, change management experts can be brought in and a change management plan created.

Deliverables

1. **Quick hit list**—Here, the e-teams identify few (usually 4–5) key process improvements that would drastically effect change. These are usually small e-initiatives that have a high impact on the bottom line and can be implemented within a short period (6–10 weeks). An example quick hit is to simplify accounts receivable terms and introduce discounts to Internet customers using credit cards.

2. **Detailed financial plan**—This plan is based on a very detailed analysis of the business processes. The previous financial analysis was done to justify the e-business project; the purpose of this analysis is to find the exact cost impacts during and when the new business changes will occur.

3. **Redesigned e-business process**—An ordering process, before it was redesigned, looked like Figure 7–8.

    This was a transformed e-business because it did not slap a Web-enabled ordering system on the front-end, but it really redesigned the way the company was doing business and changed the back-end processes, organizational structure, work culture, and reporting structure. (See Figure 7–9).

4. **Detailed implementation plan**—A detailed implementation plan with several releases should be created (see Table 7–4). The implementation plan should touch on the following aspects :

    - Scope of implementation
    - Scope of e-business processes
    - Organizational policies and procedures
    - Jobs and skills changes
    - Cultures and values
    - Information technologies
    - FTEs
    - Financial impacts at each stage

The Scope of This Project Includes Business Processes, Channel Partners, and End-Users

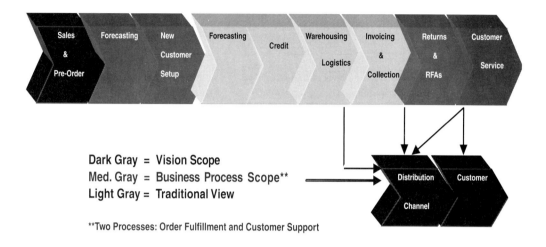

Dark Gray = Vision Scope
Med. Gray = Business Process Scope**
Light Gray = Traditional View

**Two Processes: Order Fulfillment and Customer Support

Figure 7–8   Executive summary scope of project (business process)

Table 7–4   Three Releases That Will Change an Entire Organization

Area	Release 1	Release 2	Release 3
Scope	Division 1	Division 2	Whole Organization
Business Process	End-to-end consolidation for affected scope	Warehouse, banking, transport partners involved	Dealers/channel partners fully integrated
Jobs, Skills, Organization	New organization and leadership in place	Front line hired and fully trained	Ongoing training increases skills
Management Systems	Objective, team-focused measures used	Evaluations and rewards based on results	Fully empowered front-line staff

Area	Release 1	Release 2	Release 3
Culture and Values	Team, not individual; process, not function	Best practices mindset	World class in customer intimacy
Information Technology	Continue old system acquire and install new system	Test and begin implementation of new system	Full implementation of new system
Headcount Reduction	15 positions	20 more positions	36 more positions

The New Organization of Teams Focuses on Customer Satisfaction

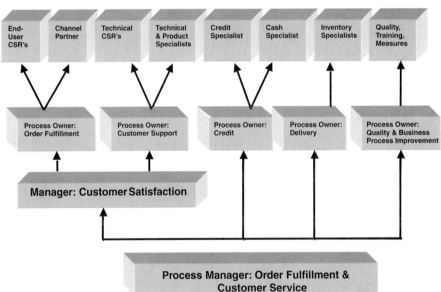

CSR = Customer Satisfaction Representatives

Figure 7–9   Organization teams focus on customer satisfaction

In the previous hypothetical HVPM case study, we did not emphasize the technology aspects; we intentionally emphasized the other aspects of e-business transformation. Many technology tasks and methodologies were used from the 4D Framework, including vendor selection, software and hardware architectures, and component-based development.

▶ Implementation Phase

The implementation phase consists of the following steps:

1. **Test organizational prototype**—This is a pilot process where the whole e-process is tested for a certain group of products and with certain selected dealers. All the aspects of the new e-business process are tested and the performance matrix is measured and fine-tuned. Communication to the whole company is a big part of this change management program.

2. **Implement full rollout**—This is where the whole redesigned process is rolled out according to the release-based rollout plan. The release-based rollout plan should be developed in an earlier phase and have high-level buy-in. Inputs from the organizational prototypes are used to fine-tune the rollout plan. The top executives must sign off on the rollout plan. Here, the change management program is in full swing, communicating, educating, explaining the benefits, and managing resistance to change.

▶ Monitoring and Maintenance Phase

In this phase, the whole change process is continuously monitored and fine-tuned for optimization. The tasks, technologies, and process matrices are measured and checked against goals on a regular basis. Senior management should be on top of the whole change. Change management tasks should be applied. Key deliverable is a Status Sheet that keeps track of the key process measurables and key communication initiatives.

8

Change Management

▶ Change Management in E-business

Change management in e-business is based on the principle that e-transformation initiatives are managed as a continuous, integrated program leading toward targeted results. An e-business change program ensures that different organizational change initiatives are aligned and that they represent a complete and coherent set of initiatives in terms of achieving targeted results (i.e., e-business goals). From now on, change management in the context of e-business will be designated as "e-change management."

The e-change management process has few components. The first one, however, involves an e-change management process that has its own definitions of change, change feasibility assessment, e-transition planning, and deployment. This process is integrated into the overall value chain management program as well as HVPM. This process, along with the specific techniques and deliverables associated with it, represent the core engine. However, e-business goals and directions often change quickly, and so to try to depict e-change management using a set of fixed processes and techniques may fail to convey the richness of experience and complexity associated with introducing large-scale change in an organization. For these reasons, we have chosen the 4D

141

Framework to consider any number of change models, allowing us to consider e-change along a number of sufficiently different and complementary perspectives.

The essential point that needs to be clearly understood is that change management is not linear in the sense that we think about on most projects. It is a complex set of interactions within a project, guided by some foundation values and rules.

A typical change process has three distinct phases as shown in Figure 8–1: unframe, transition, and reframe. In the unframe phase, the new paradigm, or new e-business model, is introduced via communication from, typically, senior management. The organization next defines the new vision with great clarity and jumps into e-transition mode. For e-business changes, this phase includes education, coaching, and leadership. Lots of e-business changes do not give enough emphasis to the interventions needed to make change happen. Even astute executives fail to estimate the amount of effort needed to transition. The third phase is the reframe, or building the new vision, phase. Here, the new concepts are inculcated and reinforced so that the change is institutionalized. Again, these phases do not follow a waterfall method; they are inherently spiral in nature.

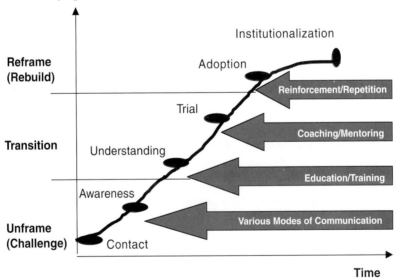

Figure 8–1   E-change management with three distinct phases

Chapter **8** | Change Management

▶ The E-Change Management Process

The e-change management process is a continuous journey to transform an organization from its current state to a targeted e-business state. It may be appropriate to consider this process as consisting of a number of levels, all of them needing to be managed to achieve the desired results.

- The first level involves processes geared toward determining how e-business results can be achieved in a specific organizational context and all of the conditions required to achieve these targeted results. This layer is directly addressed through the use of the value chain linking technique.

- The second level involves processes geared toward determining the nature and scope of the change required to achieve the targeted results. This layer requires an integration of all the e-initiatives related to achieving a targeted result in terms of the associated targeted organizational profile and an appreciation of the gap with the current organization. This layer is only partly addressed through the use of the value chain linking technique.

- The last level involves processes geared toward supporting an e-transition from the current to the targeted organization. It involves an appreciation of the relationship between the organization's change capability and resources and the specific characteristics and constraints of the change, as well as the definition and deployment of an effective e-transition approach and plan. It requires a set of change programming and deployment techniques.

All these levels have been described in Figure 8–2.

From a value chain results perspective, results and change are synergistic and should be addressed together. The magnitude of results is directly associated with the extent and magnitude of change in which the organization engages. This is illustrated in Figure 8–3 where the degree of change has a clear correlation between with the different e-transformations discussed.

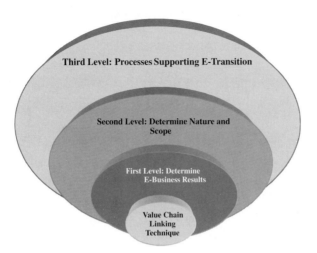

Figure 8–2   Comprehensive view of e-change management method

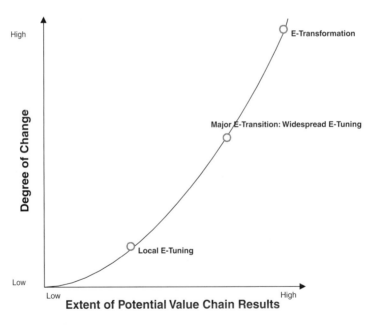

Figure 8–3   Degree of the e-change transformation categories

Chapter **8** I Change Management

Note that 75% of all organizations' transformation programs have had failures or mixed results. Of the organizations that engaged in programs that required long-term commitments, such as TQM or BPR, a fair number terminated their programs for lack of tangible results.

Why Have Organizational Transformation Initiatives (Like E-Initiatives) Failed?

The fundamental reason for e-business initiative failure is choosing no change program or choosing the wrong change management program. In fact, our experience with e-business initiatives shows that most organizations totally ignore or are unaware of the issues of change management.

Based on the basic concepts associated with value chain results and value chain linking, some of the basic limitations in implementing e-change programs could be construed in the following way:

- **Change focus is limited to immediate results**—This is the case where the change program is focused on some immediate result, such as improved quality, better customer information, or improved order-to-delivery cycle, without explicit linkages to ultimate business results. As a result, the initiative, though it may have merit in its own right, has less relevance to the business. Because the focus is on immediate results like increasing the skills of personnel or increasing service quality, without considering explicitly the results' contribution to business goals and objectives, a comprehensive plan that takes into account all the intervening factors cannot be built and ultimate results cannot necessarily be achieved.

- **Change is e-initiative-driven rather than results-driven**—Indeed, if we consider different performance improvement approaches such as downsizing, TQM, BPR, large package implementation initiatives, or even, say, an e-commerce front-end development project, these are often addressed as e-initiatives rather than as results. The focus then becomes one of implementing the initiative "the right way" as opposed to that of understanding how it relates to a given organizational context and critical organizational results. It is not enough to just do things the right way; it is critical to choose the right things to do.

- **The e-change program fails to identify all of the organization-specific changes required to support and sustain the e-business results**—Even in those cases where the different approaches are appropriately focused on ultimate e-business results, a lack of flexible adaptation of approaches to the culture of an organization does not necessarily make it possible to focus on specific changes in the organizational structure, processes, policies, practices, and people to achieve the desired results. Programmatic change tends to emphasize the common or uniform features associated with a particular approach. However, the fundamental concept that is the ultimate result of an investment is a function more of the organizational context in which the investment is deployed than the actual nature and feature of the investment. So, the organizational culture, context, policies, and structures need to be given the utmost attention.

- **The e-change program fails to deliver early results (quick hits)**— This points to the fact that a major organizational change cannot be sustained without some quick results. The results change management in e-business method, based on the value chain linking approach and technique, allows the development of an integrated change program as well as the identification of immediate value chain results that represent, in and of themselves, benefits to the organization. These results represent relevant change and performance improvement milestones within the context of the overall change program. The model then serves to identify and structure the e-initiatives associated with the realization of the different immediate results into change projects. This way, results are achieved right from the start, providing the experience, feedback, confidence, and resources early in the project to move ahead to more complex projects. This way, an organization can pursue change e-targets that are aligned with the ultimate target of the e-change program and not ignore results over the short term.

The e-change management process is designed to address these and other shortcomings associated with most e-business transformations, process improvements, and systems implementations.

E-change management relies on two distinct and interrelated components to support e-change definition, feasibility assessment, e-transition planning, and deployment: the value chain linking approach and technique, which represents the action engine of the method, and the e-change management framework, which represents the different conceptual frameworks supporting change definition, feasibility assessment, e-transition planning, and deployment.

Key Concepts and Definitions

Change management builds on the key concepts associated with the value chain analysis and linking principles and technique, which were discussed in previous chapters. However, we would like to reiterate some of the main points. The terms "results" and "value chain results" will be used synonymously.

Value chain linking represents an effective way of defining and integrating the different actions necessary to deliver an e-investment's expected results. Value chain linking integrates the different results associated with a specific e-investment. First-order results correspond to the immediate impact of an e-investment. These enable the realization of other results (e.g., immediate value chain results), leading eventually to final results for the organization. We can associate other changes that are required as a function of the different e-initiatives to these components in the value chain link for the achievement of investment-related results. Some results in the value chain link may be viewed as assets to be used to further the materialization of other parts of a value chain link. Some immediate results, along with all the e-initiatives required for their realization, may also represent natural milestones to a more comprehensive results program. Additionally, they may represent natural control points, where the costs, risks, and potential value of the whole value chain link can be formally reassessed and the e-investment direction adjusted.

The definitions follow:

- Value chain results are defined as states or properties of elements that are beyond the direct reach of an organization.

Reduced cost, improved flexibility, and increased profitability typically represent results. One of the key features of a result is that it is not within the direct reach of an organization. That is, it is not a characteristic or property that is directly actionable by the organization. A result represents the effect of a change in some of the underlying characteristics of the organizational system that has the capacity to produce a result. These changes to the characteristics of the organizational system associated with a designated result are specified by the e-initiatives associated with particular results in a value chain link.

- E-initiatives are defined as actions or elements that are under the direct reach of the organization that is targeting some e-business transformations.

E-initiatives refer to actions on organizational elements such as structures, processes, technology, operational systems and procedures, human resources (HR) policies and practices, people skills, abilities and attitudes, etc. They can also refer to actions on external elements that are within the direct reach of an organization.

Based on this distinction, the specific concepts associated with e-change management are listed below:

- Change is determined by the different sets of e-initiatives associated with the achievement of designated results. Change may involve the alteration, transformation, or substitution of any number of organizational units and organizational components as required for the realization of targeted results. These e-initiatives also represent a key input in the definition of the change program associated with a designated change.

- An e-transition includes the passage from current organizational characteristics to the organizational characteristics required to elicit the targeted e-business results. E-transition is the process of implementing the different types of e-initiatives associated with a specific change program. It includes all of the supporting and sustaining actions by which the organization can successfully implement all the different e-initiatives required to realize the change. E-transition management involves the process of managing the change projects and program required to achieve the organizational profile needed to elicit the targeted results.

▶ Value Chain Results-Based Change

The value chain link represents the action engine of the change method to the extent that it allows the identification and integration of the different organizational e-initiatives associated with a particular change. It is the element that allows the change management component in an e-business approach to be truly results-based. Underlying the results-based change management in e-business approach are numerous concepts and ideas. These concepts were discussed previously for a better understanding of the organizational aspects of e-change.

An Organization as a System

A large body of experts agree that organizations can be better understood if they are considered as dynamic, "open," and self-directed systems. As an open system, an organization can be viewed as a set of interrelated elements interacting with its environment. These elements may be viewed differently depending on the particular model used to understand and describe the organization. These may be described in terms of the various value delivery and supporting processes and functions of the organization (value chain framework), the different organizational units (organizational boundaries and relationships framework), or in terms of the different organizational elements such as strategy, processes, structure, people, technology, products, and services (organizational congruence, or fit frameworks).

It is a self-directed system to the extent that it does not passively react to its environment but rather seeks to establish a favorable position that will allow it to maintain a positive balance of input and output transactions with the environment.

Viewing the organization as a system has critical implications in terms of change and change management:

- First, change can be triggered by modifying a part or element of the system. Pragmatic change approaches often involve the introduction of change in one dimension of the organization, with scant consideration for other organizational dimensions, individual needs and perceptions, informal organizational issues, and culture. The assumption is that the other components will take care of themselves once these primary changes are introduced. This is often the case in e-business changes. Actions directed toward organizational elements tend to be the more apparent and driving components of a change program, but are often not sufficient in and of themselves for actual change to be successful.

- Second, changes in one part of the organization will have repercussions on other parts, but the different pieces will be interconnected. Therefore, in introducing a change in one part of the organization, one needs to consider the ripple effects of this change on other parts of the organization. This will ensure that the different dimensions, units, and components are properly aligned with one another and with the ultimate objectives of an organization. This entails the identification of alignment actions, which are essentially dependent on direct change e-initiatives. Failure to consider the additional alignment e-initiatives required by the change may create some unnecessary tensions between the different units and/or components of the organization and compromise the successful realization of the change.

- Third, when an event puts a system out of balance, it reacts by moving back into balance. Managing an e-transition from an initial state of balance to a new, more desirable state of balance requires other types of actions. These may include different e-mitigation and e-transition initiatives. E-mitigation initiatives address an organization's capabilities. They represent specific actions needed to make up for inadequate, insufficient, or missing resources required for the change. E-mitigation actions reduce the risks associated with the implementation of a change project or program. E-transition initiatives are actions designed to support the organization as it moves through the equilibrium imbalance-new equilibrium process. Those actions include sustaining a parallel organizational structure and operational systems as well as actions required for the management of individual reactions as the organization change program is implemented.

The identification of these different e-initiatives is based on the recognition that it may be necessary, in implementing an e-change program, to actually slow down momentarily to support individuals, mobilize organizational resources, and gain commitment to the change to move ahead more effectively in the future. Those who fail to recognize individual reactions to the change, as well as the overall capability and preparedness of the organization to implement a particular change program, will typically fail to consider the additional mitigation and e-transition initiatives required for the successful realization of the change.

Viewing the organization as a system therefore leads to the notion that change cannot be addressed fully unless it includes all of the different types of actions described above: direct actions, alignment-related actions, mitigations, and e-transition actions. Failure to consider and implement correctly any one of these different types of actions reduces the chances of success of the change program. Typically, programmatic change focuses mainly on the direct actions associated with a particular program.

E-change management, along with the value chain linking technique, supports the identification and integration of these different types of actions, making it possible to consider all those required to achieve the desired business results.

Developing Comprehensive Change Programs

Another important characteristic of a system is that different system configurations can lead to the same end. Viewing organizations as systems therefore implies that there is no single "best way" to achieve a particular result. Implications in terms of change and e-change management are as follows:

- The e-change management method, along with the value chain linking technique, support the identification of different alternatives for achieving a designated result. E-change management makes it easier to understand the distribution of e-initiatives in terms of the structural, operational, process, cultural, and technological changes as well as the nature of the resources required to support the implementation of these different e-initiatives. All unnecessary or redundant contributions to the achievement of the ultimate results, though they may have merit on their own, are not retained in the overall change program. This allows one to develop a comprehensive program based only on required e-initiatives.

- Implementing change involves risks. The results-based e-change management approach seeks to determine the optimal configuration of contributions and therefore of e-initiatives required to achieve a designated result while minimizing risk, disruption, and cost, but still focusing on the results the organization seeks to realize.

Within the results-based e-change management method, change programs and projects are defined in terms of the set of contributions that represents the least risk (cost, disruption, etc.) while allowing the organization to achieve the designated results. This allows the organization to maintain the overall effectiveness of the change program in achieving the targeted results.

Managing E-Transition as a Process

E-change management recognizes the need to identify not only those e-initiatives that will make it possible to achieve the targeted results, but also those e-initiatives required to maintain the operational activities and organizational performance throughout the e-transition period. The method provides an integrated framework for managing the different e-initiatives and change projects within an overall change program as a portfolio. It helps practitioners build a comprehensive change program around projects that are paced so they build on current organizational capabilities, deliver early results, and progressively develop the required capabilities while respecting the timeframe set for the change program. Focusing on the scope of change involved, as well as operational constraints and requirements, it supports the identification of the most appropriate implementation approach (e.g., phased vs. one-step implementation).

Change implementation requires a fine balance in terms of the situational and task-related aspects of implementing the different organizational e-initiatives on the one hand and on managing the people issues associated with change on the other hand. The situational and task-related aspects of implementing the different organizational e-initiatives lead us to think in terms of the modifications to be made to the designated organizational units or components to reach the desired results. Those that focus strictly on these aspects of change tend to assume that a change is complete once the organizational dimensions have been put in place. They ignore individual concerns and resistance or look on them as nuisances and distractions to be dismissed. Focusing overly on the people issues tends to overemphasize the political and power games associated with change and may lead to unacceptable compromises regarding the implementation of different organizational actions, rendering ultimate goals unachievable.

Those that demonstrate a balance between e-change and e-transition management are clear on the goals and changes that need to be implemented while being sensitive to the dynamics of the organization. They understand that a change cannot be complete until there is an e-transition from the old to the new organization. Though they are inflexible about their goals and targets, they are flexible in terms of their change schedule, understanding that it may be necessary sometimes to slow down for the organization and its people to adopt the proposed change. They see resistance as a normal manifestation of e-transition and encourage its open expression, recognizing that covert resistance is more detrimental to the organization (e.g., passive-aggressive behavior, sabotage, or rebellion) and much harder to deal with than overt resistance.

Multiple Models

There is no single interpretative model or framework complete enough to account for the complexity of the phenomenon and richness of the managerial experience associated with e-change management. Indeed, though there may be similarities in different cases of major organizational change, there are always a number of idiosyncratic features that set these different cases apart.

No model alone can fully explain and account for the richness of the phenomenon of organizational change. So far, it has not been possible to synthesize all the pertinent knowledge into one meta-model. Attempts to synthesize all existing models fail mostly because of an overflow in human cognitive capacities. Too much must be considered at the same time. It is realistic to consider that each approach addresses a different point of view of a complex phenomenon that has too many dimensions to be understood as a whole. One must then evolve an alternate strategy or approach. One such strategy is to develop different "points of view," or "windows," and to look at an organizational change from each of these points of view to see if something significant can be learned.

These models are:

- The best-of-breed model is best suited for understanding the scope of different change efforts.

- The organizational process model is best suited to situate a proposed or ongoing change within the framework of actions that may have already been taken, to highlight any actions that may have been omitted, and to devise an e-transition approach that will lead to successful change.

- The organizational culture model is best suited to determine the dominant culture of the organization when multiple cultures exist within the organization. Major change may then be planned to take advantage of the strengths of the organization.

- The organizational power model is best suited to evaluate the power relationships among the various participants in the e-change process and ensure that the change project has the appropriate power base to move forward.

- The change adoption model is best suited to understand the reactions of various individuals involved in a change project and to plan accordingly.

▶ E-Change Management Models

Models can be used to represent the conceptual engine of the results-driven e-change management method. Developed from the body of literature associated with strategic and large-scale organizational changes, these models provide the conceptual underpinnings for different e-change management techniques. Indeed, for each e-change management technique, we can identify one or more models that represents the conceptual underpinning for the technique. Figure 8–4 illustrates the relationship between the different models on one hand and the e-change management process and techniques on the other.

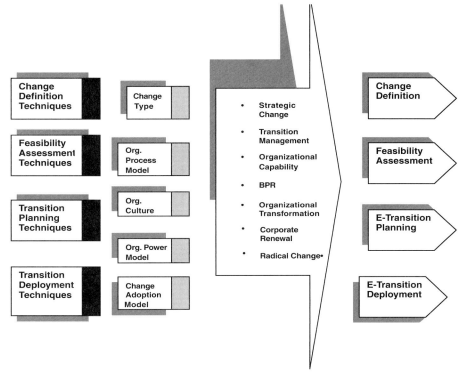

Figure 8–4 Relationships among change management models and e-change management techniques

Each model was developed with a number of criteria in mind. First, they each represent a unique and sufficiently different perspective of the change process. Second, they involve a unique set of concepts that brings value to the understanding of the change process. Third, they have immediate relevance in terms of the different phases of the e-change management process, including change definition, feasibility assessment, e-transition planning, and deployment.

The models and their relationships with the e-change management techniques provide a dynamic structure for evolving the results-driven e-change management method. Indeed, as knowledge progresses and new concepts are defined, new models can be defined in terms of the proposed criteria and used to enrich the portfolio of e-change management techniques. Conversely, the models provide a solid conceptual foundation to draw on as new e-change management techniques are required.

The framework for e-change management enables and supports the evolution of the conceptual base as well as the techniques and tools for e-change management in an integrated fashion. It also provides concrete and useful e-change management information, techniques, and tools while at the same time accounting for the diversity of organizational contexts and the diversity and complexity of issues involved in managing organizational change effectively. The use of multiple models allows the retention of rich, current scientific literature and the managerial experience on which it is based.

Best-of-Breed Model

The best-of-breed model allows the characterization of a change into one of four categories along two dimensions, that is the breadth and depth of the change, as shown in Table 8–1. It identifies four broad categories of change, each with its own characteristics, management dynamics, and requirements. It supports a rapid evaluation of a change in and of itself, based on the different e-initiatives involved in *the change*, without having to conduct an in-depth survey of the organization's past successes and failures with change or its overall change capabilities. It is based on the notion that the change implementation approach, requirements, and risks vary as functions of the type of change implied by the e-initiatives.

Table 8–1 Four Types of Change

	Local Scope	Global Scope
Fundamental Change	Major e-transition	E-transformation
Adjustments	Local e-tuning	Widespread e-tuning

The best-of-breed model represents the key model supporting the change characterization technique. It also supports the identification of resources required for an e-transition and preferred e-transition approach based on the depth and scope of the e-initiatives being considered. This model distinguishes four different types of change.

E-transformation involves a sudden modification in the working life of the members of an organization brought about to enable the adaptation of a major environmental change. It will make a major change to at least one of the core dimensions of the organization, as illustrated in Figure 8–5. It is often brought about by present or anticipated external events or forces or by a major disjunction between the organization and its environment. It is likely to cause a major disruption in the organization.

Any e-transformation generally involves the development of a new organizational vision. With this type of change, the general uncertainty of project parameters, such as delivery schedules and activity definitions, means that detailed project schedules may be unrealistic. The nature of e-transformation may be summarized as follows:

- The introduction of a different way of thinking, converging to a completely different way of doing things—so different that it was unthinkable before the change.
- Widespread restructuring, or dramatic introduction of new business lines or products.
- Revision of the mission of the organization, along with the structure, culture, place in society, and people.

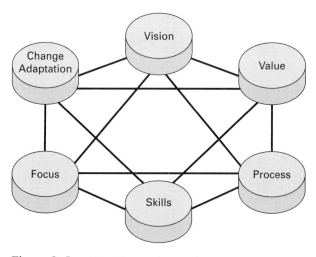

Figure 8–5   Key dimensions of an organization

- The number and complexity of cross-functional e-initiatives engages all of senior management's simultaneous attention, where the results are often in doubt, and where the e-initiatives are discussed at all levels; this is needed to maintain or advance the competitive position of the firm.

- Fundamental changes, rather than a tuning of the mission structure and operation of an organization, that change not only the "how," but the "what" and challenge the "why."

- Radical organizational change alters the fundamentals of the core business or its value set, structure, performance measurement, and reward systems; this is essential to corporate renewal.

- Broad changes that require an unsettling, or reforming of the individual's view of his or her work, his/her role, and things valued in the organization.

A major e-transition is one that involves a serious upheaval of a well-contained organizational unit. It may require the acquisition of completely new skills, the abandonment of long-standing professional practices, changes to the internal structure of the unit, changes to personnel, and other events similar to those seen in e-transformation. In this case, however, the scope of the change is limited to the organizational unit affected and little or no repercussions are observed in other parts of the organization.

A widespread e-tuning may involve the adoption of new work methods and techniques throughout the organization, but the new methods will not involve changes to elements that are considered fundamental by the organization or its members. For example, the adoption of a new standard filing system may affect all units of the organization, but not basic aspects such as the sense of belonging that members have for the organization. A widespread e-tuning might also be caused by an aggregation of a number of simultaneous superficial changes. Coordination of the implementation project will be important, but if the proposed methods are well-known and understood, there should be no major difficulties.

A fine-tuning is a local, superficial change. Such a change will not affect the entire organization, but will be limited to well-contained and identifiable departments. Improvements to methods and procedures within the mailroom of a corporation represent one example of this type of change. The change is likely to involve an adjustment of standards following the detection of errors in current practices. These changes will conform to the current logic and culture of the organization and focus on the efficiency of known operations.

A particular e-change model is determined by assessing the breadth (global, local) and depth (fundamental, adjustment) of a group of e-initiatives associated with a particular change.

The Breadth of a Change

The breadth of a group of e-initiatives determines whether a change is local or global. The value chain link documentation combined with direct observations and the judgment of the analyst provide the basis for determining the breadth of a change. A *local change* involves one or a few organizational units and has limited impact outside these units. A *global change* involves changes that are organization-wide or at least involve a number of organizational units.

The Depth of a Change

An evaluation of the depth of a group of e-initiatives will reveal whether a change reaches the core dimensions of an organization. We suggest two means of evaluation:

First approach

The first approach uses the ***six key dimensions*** of any organization (vision, value, change adaptation, processes, skills, focus—see Figure 8–5). Through the specification of guidelines and roles, vision statements inspire members and partners to concentrate on what the organization does. They create a common framework for visualizing the unsaid, the implicit, or the unprecedented. Making major changes to the mission will have a profound impact on the organization.

The identity encompasses all the parameters regulating communications between organizational leaders and external partners, as well as with the lower levels of the organization. The identity shows only what the organization wants to reveal about itself. It does not have to be complete or exact. At the strategic level, the main goal of an identity is to link an organization to a specific market. In forming a marketing strategy, the identity is used to associate the organization with groups of customers, with ways of life, or with fashions. A change of identity may thus lead clients to misunderstand the services offered or the service delivery mechanisms.

Key relationships can involve internal or external partners whose support or collaboration is essential to sustain the activities of an organizational unit or the organization as a whole. They can be major external customers or internal clients, external regulating agencies, internal staff groups, or internal or external suppliers. A change in interaction protocols with these partners may diminish their efficiency or push them to decide to abandon their support. More importantly, these partners may undertake their own e-transformation. This cannot be done without profoundly affecting the core dimensions of the organization.

The ways of work follow from a clear attribution of responsibilities, power, tasks, and resources according to an explicit set of rules and methods. Often, where they include compromises for conflict resolution, even a small change may jeopardize the overall power structure inside an organization. Where the ways of work have a long history of stability, they become an important factor of inertia, thus preventing a rapid adaptation to any e-change. New e-business initiatives typically propose fundamental changes to the ways of work.

The organizational culture is a set of values, norms, and beliefs shared by all members. Compared to a mission statement, it has more significance since its basis may stem from the very beginnings of the organization. The organizational culture may be as old as the oldest memberships of the organization. Attempts to change a culture are most often costly, disappointing, and damaging. They can never be seen as superficial changes. Because culture is strongly tied to individuals, a simpler course of action is often to put new people at the strategic levels. However, it should be considered that an organization with frequent replacement of people cannot develop a strong culture and benefit from its positive aspects.

Any project that suggests major changes to even one of these dimensions may be considered to involve e-transformation.

Second approach

A second perspective of this question has been offered by Mackenzie [1991], who compiled the hierarchy of organizational decision-making shown in Table 8–2:

Table 8–2   Hierarchy of Organizational Decision-Making[*]

Strategic Apex	Vision
	Missions
	Strategy
	Tactics
	Policies and Procedures
	Practices
	Programs/projects
	Deployment
Basic Operations	Daily Operations

[*]Mackenzie, K.D., *The Organizational Hologram: The Effective Management of Organizational Change* (New York: Kluwer Academic Publishers, 1991).

Activities closer to the top of the list are more likely to be handled by senior management. The closer an item is to the bottom of the list, the more likely the item is to be handled by a first-line supervisor. By extension, one may infer that a project involving major or fundamental change involves e-initiatives relative to items closer to the top of the list.

▶ "Nature of Change" Identification

The "nature of change" identification described here surrounds value chain results opportunities. These are determined around paths leading to targeted value chain results. The e-initiatives connected to a given value chain results opportunity make up the requirements to attain specific organizational states and results.

The best-of-breed model maps a given value chain results opportunity in terms of the breadth and depth of the e-initiatives found within it. An early understanding of the type of a change is of utmost value. It allows a rapid choice of management style and skills required. Table 8–3 shows how to classify a value chain results opportunity into one of four types. The result obtained from the change summary is used to determine the kind of e-initiative to fall in each quadrant of the best-of-breed table.

Identification will indicate whether an organizational change is fundamental or whether it will require continuous minor adjustment. The information contained in the change summary will also indicate, for example, if the majority of the organizational components required to induce the change are of a technological nature or if they mostly affect other organizational components involving business, people, and process.

Change Types

We have identified four broad types of change, each having its own specific management dynamics: major e-transition, e-transformation, local e-tuning, and widespread e-tuning.

Table 8–3   Change Types

		Breadth	
		Local Scope	Global Scope
Depth	Fundamental Change	I Major e-transition	II E-transformation
	Adjustments	III Local e-tuning	IV Widespread e-tuning

Major e-transition

A results opportunity containing a majority of e-initiatives of major depth indicates the presence of fundamental change either to the ways an organization or unit defines itself, to its ways of working, or to its relations with other units. Even if the focus of change is local, it can have an effect on other units if the changes in structure, policies, and HR required for the unit under analysis affect other units.

E-transformation

When a results opportunity contains many e-initiatives of major depth and global breadth, we say that the results opportunity involves e-transformation.

Local e-tuning change

Only when faced with a results opportunity containing results that call on e-initiatives of minor depth and local breadth can we be sure that we are in the presence of a local fine-tuning change. However, even then, we must be cautious because the cumulative impact of e-initiatives of this nature can change the workings of an organizational unit in important ways.

Widespread e-tuning

A results opportunity containing a majority of e-initiatives involving global breadth, even if they are of minor depth, will require many resources for its realization. In this case, the change is not fundamental, but important. The realization of this results opportunity will require a good deal of coordination between units. In this case, project planning is a critical condition for success. This type of change can rapidly become radical if the minor e-initiatives affect the current power status of current organizational units or functions.

To proceed with the identification, one must summarize all the e-initiatives taking place in the results opportunity. An example of such a summary is presented in Table 8–4.

This form is filled out with information contained in the value chain link documentation. The evaluation of each value chain link initiative of a given results opportunity is recorded in its respective column, as well as the results these e-initiatives contribute to. Once this summary

Table 8–4   Change Summary

E-Initiative ID	Building Block	Action-Depth	Action-Breadth
1	Technology	Major	Global
2	Technology	Minor	Local
3		Major	Global
4	HR	Major	Local
5	HR	Minor	Local
6	Process	Major	Global
7	Process	Major	Global
% of major	global e-initiatives		55%
% of major	local e-initiatives		20%
% of minor	global e-initiatives		5%
% of minor	local e-initiatives		20%

is completed, we record the results in the change type table, filling out each quadrant with its respective percentage. Table 8–5 presents a change type table filled out with the results of the previous change summary. The change type table allows for a quick assessment of the type of change associated with a results opportunity.

Table 8–5   Completed Change Types

Depth		Breadth		
		Local Scope	Global Scope	Total
Major	Fundamental Change	I 20%	II 55%	75%
Minor	Adjustments	III 20%	IV 5%	25%
	Total	40%	60%	100%

Table 8–5 shows the areas in which the e-initiatives of a given results opportunity are concentrated. In this particular example, the first con-

clusion is that the change is fundamental: 75% of the e-initiatives have a major impact. Since 55% of the e-initiatives are classified in Quadrant II, we can state that the change is also radical.

When we are in a situation where a change clearly falls in one of the four types, it is more straightforward to select the appropriate e-transition approach and take actions that will create the appropriate conditions for change.

However, if the e-initiatives are equally distributed between the four quadrants or if the majority of e-initiatives are of the adjustments type, there may be a risk of reaching the wrong conclusions and underestimating the impacts of the change. In those cases, we must consider other factors before defining the type of change.

If we take information from the descriptions of the e-initiatives, it is possible to identify the units (divisions, departments, functions, etc.) and members of the organization who are likely to be most affected by the change. For example, consider the position of a particular organization unit in its organizational context. If other units in the organization are dependent on the one affected by e-initiatives in the results opportunity, the change may be fundamental because changes within the targeted unit can affect other units.

Identifying the Resources Required for a Change

Once the type of change we are faced with has been determined, the resources required as well as the appropriate e-transition approach can be identified. The following two tables, based on research of organizational change, allow us to present the skills required to proceed with a given type of change as well as the appropriate methods to adopt for managing a given type of change.

Table 8–6 presents the key management characteristics and individual skills associated with the four types of change.

Table 8–7 shows the various management methods and characteristics appropriate to the four types of change.

The information in these tables will be helpful in quickly evaluating the feasibility of the change and will be used in the e-transition planning phase.

Table 8–6 Change Types and Key Management Skills

I	II
Skills to undertake individual coaching	Skills to assist in vision development
Skills to change others' ways of thinking	Skills to support senior management
Skills to support individual changes	Skills to manage conflicts
Skills to chair small groups	Skills to lead workgroups
Skills to manage emotional reactions	
III	**IV**
Skills to undertake individual training	Skills to design communication programs
Skills to design and present methods	Skills to undertake group coordination
Knowledge of the work of the organization	Skills to design training programs
	Skills to support users

Table 8–7 Change Types and Change Project Management

I	II
Change is hard to program	Change cannot be programmed
Progress must be re-evaluated often	Phases managed with different techniques
Those affected directly influence the change	Senior management support essential
Success requires great focus	Legitimized by involvement in workgroups
	May take several years
III	**IV**
Change may be programmed	Change may be programmed
Technical questions dominate	Duration depends on numbers affected
Project management needed	Success requires management controls

Organizational Process Model

The organizational process model in the context of the 4D Framework identifies four generic phases of change, along with the key activities and results associated with each phase. The successful completion of these phases is all the more important when the change under consideration is fundamental. This model will allow a practitioner to situate a proposed or ongoing change within the framework of actions that may have already been taken, to highlight any actions that may have been omitted, and to devise an e-transition approach that will lead to successful change.

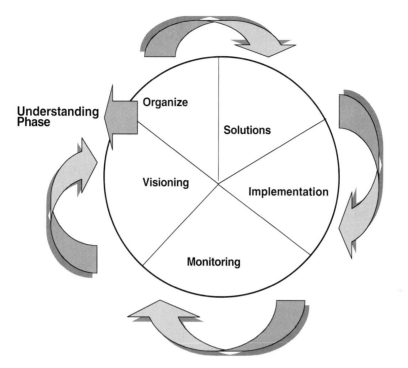

Figure 8–6   The organizational process model of e-change management

Figure 8–6 illustrates the four phases of a change process, ranging from the conceptual to post-implementation maintenance. The four phases are: understanding, solutions, implementation, and monitoring. The understanding phase has two sub-phases: visioning and organizing. The process normally starts with vision development and may require multiple iterations. Figure 8–6 shows the phases in a non-linear pattern, because of the dynamic nature of the e-change management.

Visioning

The objective of this phase is to produce a clear statement of the desired state of the key components of the organization at a future point. This phase may commence when an individual member of the organization detects a potential dysfunction within the organization or in its relations with the business environment. There may be few warning signals and the sponsor of the vision will often act alone for some time as champion of the idea. The major challenge will be to verbalize the vision in such a way to successfully communicate it to organizational associates.

The vision must be based on a sound organizational and environmental diagnosis, as well as point out the general direction in which the organization must move and the targets that must be met. Since a major change project will be seen as disruptive by at least some members of the organization, one of the purposes of the vision is to provide meaning to the change during the period of e-transition. It should also serve to sustain the organization's resolve as it goes through the stress and turbulence of the change.

At the end of this phase, the need for change should be felt throughout the organization, and an explicit vision statement and change agenda should be communicated to other members of the organization so that they will understand and support it. In the case of major change, some of the outputs of this phase include a compelling case for change and a change agenda. The case for change is designed to communicate the need for change. It should include a brief description of the business context, the current business opportunity or source of concern, the current or anticipated market demand, the shortcomings of the organization in meeting such a demand, and the consequences of inaction. The change agenda should highlight the "vital few" results that will provide the foundation, or reference point, of the change, a general map of what the future organization will look like, as well as the key streams of activity that will lead the organization from the current to the targeted state.

If the vision development phase has not been completed successfully, the need as well as direction and meaning of the change will be unclear to at least some members of the organization. It will then be difficult or impossible to accomplish the next phase of the process, which is legitimization.

Organizing

The principal aim of this phase is to obtain the resources necessary for the operationalization of the vision and its attainment. For this to happen, one must identify the main stakeholders, analyze the power relationships among them, and manage whatever negotiations are required, as well as any conflicts that arise, to build a committed and efficient team of senior change managers.

Note that during this phase, multiple organizational defenses may be raised and negotiations may languish. An important risk is that some stakeholders may ask for detailed plans before agreeing to commit to the change. One of the critical errors at this phase of the process is over-specification. Indeed, the preparation of detailed plans is often unproductive at this stage. The senior change managers must avoid such time-consuming activities at this point. The vision cannot be a detailed plan, but rather should involve an espousal of the direction and targets of the change and an agreement to plan further.

Should the legitimization phase be omitted or not completed, the consultant will often observe anything from a lack of buy-in, to the development of an active defense against the change. Activity-based change programs, where senior change managers simply go through the different meetings and rituals associated with a particular change initiative without changing their day-to-day behavior, represent one indication of a lack of buy-in. One may also observe attempts to take over the change project and divert it to other ends or even to return to past practices. If the project is pushed to the next phase, one will then find that the required resources have not really been committed, that they are not available, and the implementation will eventually fail.

Solution

The objective of this phase is to translate the vision statement and detail the change agenda to produce operational goals, tasks, and organizational structures that are essential to implementing the change. One must also define an e-change management structure that includes the range of personnel whose participation is required. The major components of this phase are:

- Identification of the tasks necessary for e-change management
- Creation of e-change management structures and work teams
- Identification of specific architectures and goals aligned with a vision
- Commitment to the vision of a broader segment of the organization

A completed solution phase will produce an implementation plan aligned with the general direction and targets of the vision and make use of the resources and support obtained in the legitimization phase.

Should the Solution phase be omitted or not completed, implementation will be difficult and the risk of failure will increase. The plan will be expressed in terms that are too general or ill-adapted to one or more parts of the organization. The managers of the change project may be tempted to fall back on "programmatic change," which is the application of generic techniques and approaches such as TQM, management by objectives, and training, without explicit linkage to specific targets of the vision.

Implementation

The aim of the implementation phase is to make modifications to the organizational structures, tasks, ways of work, and reward structure to reduce the risk of failure and improve the probability of success. The changes to organizational structures deal mainly with power redistribution among members of the organization. The main objective of modifying the tasks, ways of work, and reward structure is to generate new behaviors consistent with the vision statement.

The implementation phase must deal with the nuts and bolts of the plan developed in the previous phase. It requires the precise identification of norms and rewards, technical training, and technological needs. It is important to explicitly address the issues of work organization, communication channels, and lines of authority. This detailed plan must take into account whatever local variations are required across the organization.

During the implementation phase, the old organization, complete with reporting relationships, accountabilities, and output, continues to exist while the new organization is actually being put in place. For a period of time, there may be a requirement for dual organizations to run side-by-side, creating the need to design interim e-transition structures, systems, and policies to support the transition from the current to the targeted state.

Should implementation be rushed or superficial, problems are likely to arise when attempts are made to change power distribution, negotiate a new reward structure, or experiment with new client/supplier practices. If there is no power shift from the current structural arrangements to the structures and processes underlying the target organization, the old organization will win by default. It is therefore important to align authority with responsibility, reward structure with performance evaluation, and conflict resolution practices with targeted structures. The follow-up phase is of utmost importance, ensuring that the transition is going forward and that the organization does not swing back to old cultural habits.

Important Ideas

In this section we will present some important organizational culture and e-change issues that one needs to be aware of.

Flexibility vs. controlling

Organizations can range from great flexibility to tight control. If an organizational culture has a focus on flexibility, it places emphasis on organic processes, individuality, spontaneity, and innovation; if an organizational culture has a focus on tight control, it emphasizes the achievement of short-term goals, stability, rules, and procedures.

Internal vs. external

Organizations can be either internally or externally focused. In an organization with an internal focus, internal coordination and integration activities are most important; in an organization with an external focus, one will see that market competition and differentiation activities like planning, competitive analysis, and marketing are most important.

Team culture

A team culture places individuals, personal development, participation, and team-building before procedures, structure, and economic considerations. An organization may have adopted this position if, in the past, it has been able to respond to environmental pressures through an enhancement of collaboration and communication among its members. Such an organization will seek to use individual commitment and the development of human potential as the main responses to environmental uncertainty.

Entrepreneurship

An entrepreneurship culture places a premium on individual achievement through creativity and personal initiative. Individual achievement will often be measured in economic or organizational growth and development. This culture will often be found in young organizations operating in a new, growing, and active market. A premium will be placed on the ability to find new resources, detect new opportunities, take risks, and be innovative.

Rational management

The rational management culture favors the development of efficient production. It is based on furnishing goods and services of a specified quality for the lowest possible cost. The organizational strategy focuses on exploiting competitive advantage and market superiority. This culture will often be found in mature organizations offering goods and services in a stable market. A premium will be placed on the ability to develop a production process and control costs rather than on product innovation.

Formal hierarchy

The formal hierarchy culture favors long-established rules, methods, and power structures. Such an organization will often have a long history of success in a relatively stable environment. The rules, methods, and power structures eventually come to be seen as part of the reason for the success of the organization. Energy will be spent to polish and refine them, but their existence will not be called into question. Often, external demand may fluctuate, but the dominant position of the organization will allow it to maintain its internal ways and habits. This culture will often be found in large firms that dominate their markets, in state enterprises, in public utilities, and in government ministries.

The nature of an organizational culture may be readily determined based on interviews and questionnaires. For senior management, these observations can be gathered from informal interviews and observations over a period of time. If necessary, a questionnaire can be developed to obtain data from other management and working levels. In many cases, experienced practitioners should be able to describe the culture of an organization without using formal data collection procedures such as questionnaires and structured interviews.

Note that it is likely that a change project based on a cultural model inconsistent from that which dominates the organization will give rise to misunderstandings, is more likely to create resistance and conflicts, and is inherently more risky. Indeed, culture can be an important contributor to the organizational inertia that delays or prevents change. It provides the foundation for identifying different e-transition planning and deployment approaches, based on the degree of compatibility of a change with the prevailing culture.

Organizational Power Model

The organizational power model is of use in evaluating the feasibility of a proposed change. This model supports the evaluation of power dynamics between the various participants in a change. The model also provides indications in terms of assessing and putting in place an appropriate power base for the successful implementation of a change.

Experts who believe in this model have referred to three sources of power: formal power, individual power, and departmental power (see Figure 8–7). The following section presents these different components of organizational power along with their effect on the change process.

Power is often defined as the capacity to influence another person or group to accept one's own ideas or plan. It determines the ability to exercise social influence to achieve a goal. Popular notions that treat power as a game or contest among individuals should be set aside in this discussion.

Those controlling the resources required for organizational change are called *agents*. Those providing resources to support change are called *sponsors*. Agents, their roles, and their commitment to a change must be identified as soon as possible to allow for evaluation of the availability of required resources.

Power management becomes central within the context of a change project. Power is used to acquire the resources required to effect the change. Some agents may not be under the direct authority of the change sponsor. In these cases, these agents must use their own power to achieve change goals they may not have defined themselves.

Figure 8–7   Elements of organizational power

Formal power

Formal power is closely linked to the formal structure of an organization. It derives from the position described by a job title and from the job's description and responsibilities. It gives the formal authority required to exert control over designated resources, including one's subordinates. Formal power operates through the authority that gives direct control over human and material resources. Control over human resources gives individuals with authority the means to distribute rewards and punishment to people they are responsible for. This is commonly referred to as *downward power*.

Formal power is exercised through the organizational structure. Centralized organizations tend to support formal power, while flatter or less structured organizations tend to limit it. Formal power is of little value when trading or negotiating with peers, with people in higher level positions, or with individuals in unrelated departments. Other forms of power must be exercised in these circumstances.

Individual power

Individuals who do not have formal power may still manage to influence decisions and control resources. Such individual power, or influence, is based on personal characteristics and is exercised through other members of the organization. It is based on abilities and background experiences linked to the individual and not to the organizational position. The potential power bases that can contribute to individual power are grouped into three categories: knowledge, personality, and networking.

Departmental power

Departmental power is the ability of a department to influence other workgroups through actions that may or may not be within its formal task assignment. We list three sources of departmental power:

- **Need-based**—A department may assume pressing organizational needs that would not be otherwise covered.
- **Information-based**—A department may provide information that it has gleaned on markets, competitors, products, or regulations and which is not available from other sources.
- **Skill-based**—A department may have skills that cannot be replaced or circumvented by other workgroups.

One may see the emergence of needs-based power, for example, when market conditions are rapidly changing or when there is a series of resignations of key people elsewhere in the organization. A department may obtain this kind of power by accepting to carry the heavier load that results. Sales and marketing divisions with external sources of information, for example, may hold information-based power. In the case of a change project, the project team is likely to have information and resources not available to others and will be seen to have information-based power by others. Skill-based power is often held by professional workgroups who not only have the knowledge but also a legal status that allows them alone to perform certain functions.

The power relationships between the people and departments involved in a change represent a key dimension affecting the feasibility of a change. One method of considering the different power relationships is through a power map of the organization. An example of a power map is shown in Figure 8–8. The power map is complex and demonstrates that power is a relative rather than an absolute attribute.

As can be seen from the illustration, one can identify seven main power relationships:

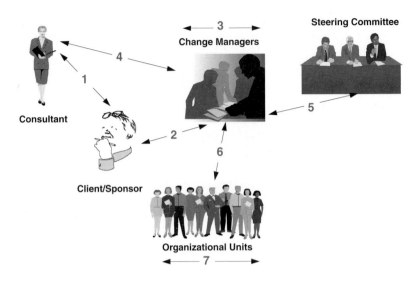

Figure 8–8   The power map

- The relationship between the consultant and the client/sponsor
- The relationship between the client/sponsor and the group of change managers
- The relationships among the members of the group of change managers
- The relationship between the consultant and the group of change managers
- The relationship between the group of change managers and the board or other governing body
- The relationship between the group of change managers and the department managers and departments

For the individuals and workgroups involved in a change project, a consultant can prepare a power map using Tables 8–8 and 8–9 as a guide for describing power relationships.

Table 8–8 Factors in Individual Power

Factor	Example
Knowledge: Expertise	An individual may gain power through knowledge obtained by training or experience.
Knowledge: Information	An individual may gain power from a capacity to obtain, retain, distribute, or even distort information.
Knowledge: Tradition	An individual may gain power through the seniority that confers knowledge of the values and culture of the organization.
Personality: Charisma	An individual may gain power through an ability to communicate his or her model and energize others.
Personality: Reputation	An individual may gain power through his or her known track record, which may be based on documented facts or rumors.
Personality: Professional Credibility	An individual may gain power through a professional status derived from an external governing body.
Networking: Political Access	An individual may gain power by calling on an internal social network, giving access to key individuals.
Networking: Staff Support	An individual may gain power by calling on the internal social network of subordinates who collaborate because they too will benefit.

Table 8–9 Factors in Departmental Power

Factor	Example
Uncertainty	A department can provide information on markets or clients to reduce uncertainty.
Substitutability	A department will have power if no other department in the organization can perform its functions or activities.
Centrality	A department will have power if it has a critical position in the workflow that renders other departments dependent.

Implementing the E-Change Management Process

This chapter describes the process associated with the value chain results-driven e-change management method. It involves a generic e-change management process as well as a set of e-change management techniques designed to support this process.

▶ The Value Chain Results Management Cycle

The process for e-change management is defined in terms of the phases of the value chain results management cycle. Activities of the e-change management process will be part of the value chain results management cycle. Depending on the nature of the assignment or specific problem and issue at hand, only the events associated with the management process or organizations choose to follow the activities and perform the activities required for the e-change management process without jeopardizing the change management initiatives and activities.

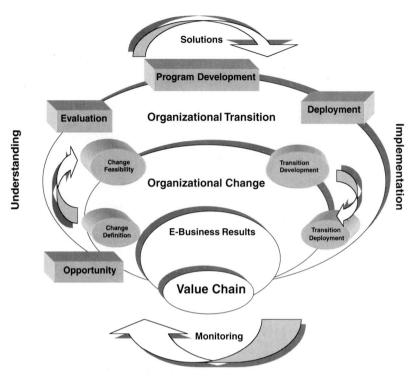

Figure 9-1   4D e-change management process

Figure 9-1 describes the position of the e-change management process relative to the value chain results management cycle.

Activities represent key steps in the process. Participants represent the key deliverables required by or resulting from an activity, or supporting techniques and tools to be used to produce related deliverables.

Though it is presented as a linear process, it should be clearly understood that the actual application of the e-change management process will be mostly iterative. In fact, the activities and steps in the process and the targeted results may change rapidly. This will definitely give the process a non-linear characteristic that would need non-linear thinking and management philosophies.

E-Change Understanding Phase

The organizational e-change understanding and assessment phase focuses on the identification of the change activities required in the current organization to realize a designated value chain results opportunity. It minimizes the scope of organizational changes and makes sure that all change activities follow the change alignment principle. However, it does not at this stage address the organization's change resources, capabilities, timelines or e-transition issues.

Objectives

The objectives of the e-change understanding phase are:

- Determine the scope of the organizational change related to a relevant value chain results link
- Identify the resources required and understand their importance in order to implement the change
- Contribute to the deliverables of the change assessment and e-transition understanding phases

Types of changes

Based on a heuristic evaluation of individual e-initiatives, the organizational change understanding phase helps identify the type of organizational change an organization will face as it chooses a particular value chain results opportunity.

There are four broad types of organizational change: major e-transition, e-transformation, local e-tuning, and widespread e-tuning. Each type of organizational change requires different skills as well as management methods. This phase ensures that a sound diagnostic of the scope of the organizational change is made, allowing for the identification of resources and adoption of methods that will support a smooth e-transition from a as-is to a targeted state.

E-Change Assessment Phase

It is at the e-change assessment phase that the organization's change capability and resources are addressed and considered. Strategies include detail analysis of resources and organizational cultures and if the resources required for the proposed organizational changes not be available, the strategies will address those issues. These may involve some modifications in the proposed e-initiatives, some changes to e-initiatives included in a value chain results opportunity, or the identification of alternative paths toward the chosen ultimate result.

E-Transition Solutions Phase

In the e-transition solutions phase of the 4D Framework, e-transition requirements and issues are addressed. E-transition issues may encompass any or all costs or constraints, be they of an economical, logistics, political, or personal nature associated with the change, including specific requirements to sustain operations while the change occurs. E-transition requirements involve all of the actions required for a successful e-transition to occur. Though most of these requirements may have been indirectly addressed in previous phases, the development of an e-transition plan is most likely going to uncover new, unforeseen e-transition requirements, costs, or constraints.

E-Change Implementation Phase

In the implementation phase, modifications to organizational structures, tasks, work flows, and incentive structures are actually realized in such a way as to reduce the risk of failure and improve the probability of success of the change program. Modifications to organizational structures ensure redistribution of power among employees and managers of the organization. The main objective of modifications to the tasks, work flows, and incentive structures is to inculcate new behaviors consistent with the change definition statement that is usually denied in the understanding phase.

In large organizations, this can be a very complex task. The e-change implementation phase must deal with the details of change defined during the understanding phase. It requires the detail identification of norms, incentives, technical training, and technological needs. It is important to explicitly address the issues of work, organizational structures, communication channels, power structures, and lines of authority. This detailed plan must take into account whatever local e-change issues (geographical, cultural) are required as well as enterprise wide and cross enterprise issues.

▶ Methods

The methods and guidelines can be used to ensure that all the e-initiatives linked to a given value chain result(s) have been identified and documented appropriately. A documentation standard for the different value chain link components is also outlined in this section. The documentation provides detail information on the targeted goals of an organization and the various means to attain them.

Generation Methods

This section presents the guidelines and techniques used to generate additional e-initiatives. It involves the following elements: First, it proposes a standard approach for considering the different components of the organization as well as the relationships among them. Second, it presents guidelines in terms of the generation of the different additional e-initiatives that represent the key influencing points around a particular result. Third, it provides guidelines for ensuring that the additional e-initiatives generated are comprehensive and follow change alignment principle. They must be congruent with one another and aligned to organizational goals.

Change alignment principle

The change alignment principle was developed after doing thorough analysis of successful companies. There has been a large number of studies that show that successful organizations are characterized by organizational building blocks (defined in previous chapters) aligned with one another. Effective organizations have devised their organizational building blocks and their interrelationships so they are in a state of dynamic equilibrium. This equilibrium comes from change alignment between organizational components interacting with each other. Alignment means that the organizational structures, systems, workflows and people of interrelated organizational components support and enhance each other.

This principle ensures that a targeted result needs to be achieved while maintaining an the daily operations and the current strategies of the organization. It is like designing while doing, changing car parts while driving. The challenge here is to determine how a given result can be

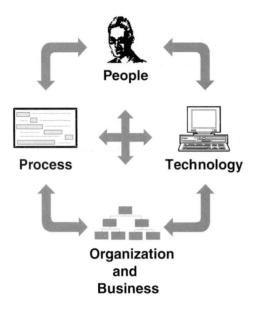

Figure 9–2 The e-organization relationship

achieved from the dynamics of different organizational building blocks, which building blocks and their interrelationships are critical to achieve the value chain results, and how those changes in organizational structures will affect other organizational units. This principle ensures that when value chain results require changes in one organizational building blocks, the attributes, and contributions of other organizational building blocks related to the one being changed have to be assessed and adapted. The foundation principle is that all building blocks (people, process, business) and e-initiatives must be in alignment and reinforce each other's objects, in order to attain the final value chain result.

We have talked about the four fundamental building blocks (components). In Figure 9–2, the illustration shows these four class blocks and their mutual relationships. Those relationships reinforces the fact that a change in one or many of these building blocks will have an impact on other related building blocks. People, process, organizational structure, technology are related and any e-business value chain result must be attained via the mutual alignment of all these components.

Each class refers to a specific organizational building block (component):

- **Business (organization)**—Refers to the hierarchical structure and division of work and job tasks, formal and informal administrative rules, control and coordination mechanisms, as well as methods and procedures at the organization and job levels. Organizational structures are used to identify the locus of power coming from formal authority.

  Formal administrative rules, methods, and procedures are explicitly stated and formally developed. Often, they are written and can be referred to.

  Informal rules and procedures are those that have emerged to complement or bypass formal rules and procedures. These informal rules and procedures are often more important in explaining the current organizational performance and must be taken into account.

- **People**—Refers to administrative policies, rules, and procedures concerning the management of human resources. Appraisal and reward systems, recruiting, and training policies and practices would also be found under this class of components.

- **Process**—Refers to an organized use of technology and workflow for the generation of goods and services. It may also include the scheduling methods and programming rules in use and plant layout, as well as the quality norms used to measure process performance.

- **Technology**—Refers to the set of tools used for production of goods and services. Technology may affect the design of work processes, work tasks, and workers' expertise, as well as the range of administrative mechanisms that can be used to control and coordinate tasks.

Identifying key change initiatives

Additional e-initiatives involve change in an organizational component associated with a given pair of components on the path of a value chain link model. Additional e-initiatives are actions taken on specific organizational components to achieve a result. Targeted Value chain results can be obtained by modifying, adding, or eliminating organizational building blocks.

Using the value chain linking technique, there are two ways to generate additional e-initiatives: one is by defining precisely the components in a value chain link model, the other is by analyzing the relationships between two successive value chain link components on a path.

The second approach for generating additional e-initiatives involves the analysis of any pair of value chain link components on a value chain link path. A pair of value chain link components is composed either of two successive value chain results or an e-initiative followed by a result. The last component of a pair is always a result. The guidelines offered by the change alignment principle help identify the intervening organizational components and appropriate actions to reach organizational goals as determined by the value chain link.

Focusing on the value chain link components, the following questions can be addressed:

1. How does the first value chain link component influence the achievement of the next result?

2. What additional e-change(s) initiative(s) need(s) to occur for this result to be reached?

3. What organizational components are involved in these changes? What characteristics do these organizational components need to demonstrate to generate a given result? What modifications need to be made to the organizational components that have been identified? What impacts do modifications to these organizational components have on other related organizational components?

Intermediate value chain results are not sufficient in and of themselves to achieve successive result(s) on a value chain link map. Other actions must be taken involving different components to achieve a result. The guidelines following from the change alignment principle will help identify the related building blocks, which may otherwise be totally ignored in a linear analysis.

The change alignment principle

This model ensures that all the different classes of organizational 4 D building blocks (components) have been considered and that all the appropriate additional e-initiatives have been identified. Generally, organizational components in all the different categories of the work environment are called on to maintain change alignment while focusing on a specific result. The magnitude of the required modifications of each organizational component is a function of: the attributes of the current components, the required state, and the relationships between organizational components involved in a targeted organizational profile. Take the example of "increased flexibility," a result achieved following the implementation of an e-design system. An e-design system is a collaborative design tool used by globally located product designers who use Web-based collaborative systems. Figure 9–3 illustrates the impacts this change in technology has on different organizational components.

Figure 9–3 shows that to increase flexibility at the manufacturing level, an initial change involving a technology component, an e-supply chain, was considered. However, this investment alone was not sufficient to attain the desired result. Modification to organizational components related to technology had to be sustained by adaptation to other organizational components. Other classes of organizational components had to be modified; for instance, components related to structure modified responsibilities and job tasks and components related to HR adapted the compensation policy and training program to the requirements of the technology, along with modifying components of the process involving changes to plant layout. The principle of internal fit or congruence is very helpful to identify the e-initiatives that must be

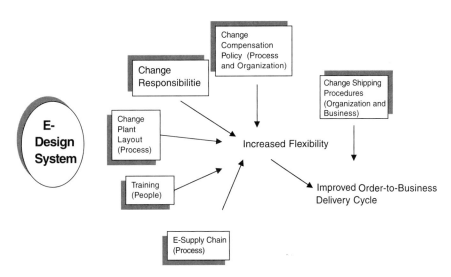

Figure 9–3   Application of the internal change principle within the value chain link approach.

taken to attain value chain results. Table 9–1 provides useful questions for identifying additional e-initiatives following changes in any particular organizational component.

Table 9–1 Questions Supporting the Identification of Additional E-Initiatives

Classes	Considerations	Leading Questions
Technology	A prime determinant of organizational improvement	• What are the results sought by the technology? • How will this technology contribute to this result? • What are the requirements of the technology? • What impacts will this technology have on other aspects of the organization? • How will this technology affect the organization
Business (Organization)	Types of organization policies, procedures, and methods	• Do current structural components support the achievement of the targeted result? • Are there any modifications to the formal authority, the existing policies and procedures required for the achievement of a result? • What modifications have to be made to the responsibilities and job tasks to achieve a result? • What modifications to the control and coordination mechanisms need to be carried out to reach a result? • What impacts do these modifications to structural components have on other organizational components?
Process	Organized uses of technology for generation of goods and services	• What modifications to the current process design will contribute to the attainment of a result? • Do we have to change the workflow principles, rules, and scheduling methods? • What impacts do these modifications to the processes have on other organizational components?
People	Motivation, incentives, and competence	• What expertise and knowledge are required? • Is training required to achieve a result? • What modifications to the reward system are needed? • What impacts do these modifications to HR components have on other organizational components?

▶ Recording and Documentation (An Important Deliverable)

A value chain link model describes the targeted states of an organization given its specific organizational context and external environment. In this section, we suggest a standard for recording and documentation that keeps track of information pertaining to an as-is organizational state as well a future state. The standard suggested allows for structured information as well as some value added free form information.

Value Chain Results

Value chain results are defined as a state or property of elements that are beyond the direct reach of an organization. A property is perceived as an immediate or final requirement for an organization to successfully implement an investment and achieve value chain results.

The documentation of each value chain result contains a summary description of the result. This description should contain the current as well as the future properties of an organization, its units, and/or components. This helps in identifying the gaps between as-is and targeted organizational states. In turn, it will also be used for generating additional e-initiatives.

Examples of value chain results include improved flexibility, increased efficiency, improved product/service quality, improved product design, etc. Each value chain result has a particular meaning according to a given organizational context and must be described accordingly. Take, for example, the result "improved flexibility." The dictionary definition of flexibility is the capability to adapt easily to different situations without breaking. However, it can take on different meanings according to different organizational contexts. It can mean that a company wants to produce and sell a greater variety of products, or it may mean it wants to deliver orders more rapidly, or it can mean that it can adapt its products to the evolving needs of its customers. Each of the above describes different characteristics of flexibility. The right description has to be set f=for a given organization's goals and culture. Once the description is set, the different components that can support the achievement of the targeted result can be defined and aligned.

If the YXZ Company describes flexibility as the capability of manufacturing a greater variety of products on the same manufacturing line, then the attributes of flexibility for this company must be defined the same way.

The as-is state and the targeted state both need to be described in the documentation using the same characteristics.

Consider the previous example, where the result "improved flexibility" was described as the capability to produce different products on the same manufacturing line. Here, the description of the as-is state should refer to the same parameters as those used to describe the targeted state of improved flexibility. A list of important information, such as the current production capacity, number of employees, productivity by employee, manufacturing technology, workflow, work tasks, etc., need to added depending on the depth of analysis required. This information can be used eventually for different purposes such as cost/benefit evaluations, identifying additional e-initiatives, assessing resources needed to achieve the targeted result, etc.

Figure 9–4 provides a template for documenting value chain results. The information to include in the documentation can vary as a function of the nature and objectives of an assignment; however, to have a meaningful and valid model, the targeted and as-is states of the value chain results as well as their relevant attributes must be documented. All other information may be helpful, but it may be optional. The proposed template for documenting the targeted and as-is states of results also includes space for adding information concerning the organizational unit(s) that will be affected and/or will contribute to the achievement of a result.

Documenting E-Initiatives

The documentation of each e-initiative contains a narrative summary description of the initiative. This summary provides the basis of the e-change management method. For each e-initiative, the documentation will record the action that is being taken and the organizational component that will be affected. The summary description of an e-initiative should include the following basic information: the e-initiative name,

Outcome: Improved Flexibility	ID Number:
Summary Description:	
Desired/Expected State:	
Flexibility means producing a greater variety of products using the same manufacturing line.	
Current State:	
The company manufactures only one product (description) on one manufacturing line. Production capacity used is 50%. The current productivity is X products/hour, etc.	
Units Concerned:	
Manufacturing Department Others	

Figure 9–4   Template for documenting value chain results

the reference number used in the value chain link model, and a brief and explicit statement of expected value chain results.

Beyond this basic information, the description should state the action that the e-initiative involves, the organizational component of this action, and an identification of the organizational units (divisions, departments, function, etc.) affected by the e-initiative. The description should present the current nature of the organizational component that is to be changed by the e-initiative and the targeted or expected effect on this organizational component.

The information may be recorded on standard forms of an appropriate design or in a database. Figure 9–5 illustrates a template that may be used to record the information described in this section.

Looking at the proposed template for documenting e-initiatives, one can see that the organizational components affected by an e-initiative are classified using the classes of the work environment model presented in Figure 9–5. E-initiatives are also classified by how they affect an organization.

Initiative:		ID Number:	
Summary Description:		**Component Class:**	
Desired State and Results:		Business	
		People	
		Process	
		Technology	
		Depth:	
Current State and Results:		Major	
		Minor	
		Breadth:	
		Global	
		Local	

Figure 9–5   Template for documenting e-initiatives.

Classifying E-Initiatives

The documentation should contain all of the information to facilitate the characterization of the change required to achieve a targeted result. This includes:

- **A classification of the organizational component(s) affected by the initiative**—This involves an entity of the organization, or of its immediate environment, that may be manipulated and whose substance may be modified by actions of those within the organization.

- **A classification of the action**—An action will modify the properties of a component, create a new component, or eliminate an existing one.

This classification of components is done following the four classes of building blocks in the 4D Framework methodology presented in previous chapters. Each class refers to different organizational components.

Table 9–2 gives a description of each class of components and provides several examples to help in the classification process.

Table 9–2   Organizational Component Classes

Class	Description	Examples
Organization/Business	Legal and hierarchical structure and consequent division of work, administrative rules, procedures, and systems	Number of organizational levels, authority distribution, management control systems, administrative techniques, standards, jobs tasks and requirements, and control and coordination systems
People	Expertise, skills, knowledge, and formal and informal power of individuals	Reward systems, performance assessment, training, job enrichment, and recruitment system
Process	Organized uses of resources for the generation of goods and services	Process design, scheduling methods, priority systems, quality norms, and programming rules
Technology	The set of tools and machines used for production of goods and services	Computers, networks, software (MRP, CASE, spreadsheets), data banks, machine tools and manufacturing cells, and choice of materials

Evaluating E-Initiatives: Depth and Breadth

As shown on the template used for documenting e-initiatives, the impact of each e-initiative on the organizational components it affects must be evaluated and recorded. This evaluation will be used to characterize the type of change associated with a value chain results opportunity.

Evaluating the depth of e-initiatives

The depth of an e-initiative is classified as minor or major according to the assessment of its anticipated impacts. A major impact will modify the identity of a component and its basic characteristics or workings. A major impact may change the fundamental orientation of the whole organization (including its vision, mission, identity, or culture). An e-initiative involving a minor impact will modify properties of the component without changing its basic nature. A minor e-initiative is typically limited to changes in practices, rules, and instructions associated with day-to-day management.

Evaluating the breadth of e-initiatives

The breadth of an e-initiative refers to the number and diversity of organizational units and/or individuals affected by the e-initiative. The breadth of an e-initiative can be classified as local or global according to the subjective assessment of its anticipated impacts. An action may be considered local if it affects few units or individuals across the organization or if its effects are limited to the majority of members of a few small organizational units. An action may be considered global when it affects the majority of the members of an organization across all units.

10

Case Study: Fictitious ABC Company

Now that we have studied all the ingredients of the 4D Framework for e-business, let's mix them together and see what comes out. In this chapter, we will explore a hypothetical organization as it grapples with its own e-initiatives and see how it employs the 4D Framework to realize its own e-business potential.

▶ Problem Definition

Vendor S has been actively involved with ABC over the past year, building relationships and understanding ABC's business, applications, and technology requirements. ABC is changing its procurement from a mainframe, EDI–based system to a Web-enabled, Ariba-based system.

The two sides decide that they need to "crawl" first before they can walk. They agree on a phased approach to the project. In Phase 1, the companies agree to do key product fulfillment and rapid shipment—where a combination of basic cataloguing and EDI are agreed on for specific high-value products. Vendor S agrees to change its internal processes and even reshuffle organizational structures to support the rapid shipment of the agreed-upon product sets. In Phase 2, departments of ABC will customize a full-blown customer catalog for all products. In Phase 3, they agree on true e-commerce using sophisticated Web EDI, with Web-enabled B2B transactions in the context of an IPE structure previously agreed on. Processes on both sides of the fence will need to be changed.

Vendor S has changed its systems to be Web-enabled and already has an e-commerce-based order entry system (Oracle) in place. This system is designed to handle procurement from Ariba, Commerce One, Netscape, Intellysis, and traditional EDI. The major issue is to integrate the two.

▶ Solution

In the understanding phase, the Vendor S account manager establishes initial contacts with ABC's technical staff and business personnel. Vendor S is convinced very early on that it has definite solutions for ABC's e-procurement needs. After this initial decision to go, the two companies agree to create a framework of "things" that cover business analysis and technical analysis (including package interfaces that need to be developed), develop a high-level rollout road map and then a plan, agree to some common e-project management tasks like status meetings and their formats, and conduct a kickoff meeting. They jointly discuss with Ariba their rollout plan, so that it matches with the business plans of both companies.

In the solutions phase, Vendor S initially establishes a project team to understand in detail ABC's business, culture, policies, and procedures, as well as the technology-related requirements. Vendor S conducts several interviews of key people within ABC's information systems (IS) organization and procurement division. As a result of these interviews, Vendor S becomes aware of the e-procurement system's detailed requirements. Company ABC has no single procurement division; each business unit has its own procurement. So, ABC and Vendor S decide that this transition will be continuous and will take a few years to be final and complete. Hence, they create a program office rather than just a project team. Program managers and project managers (PMs) from

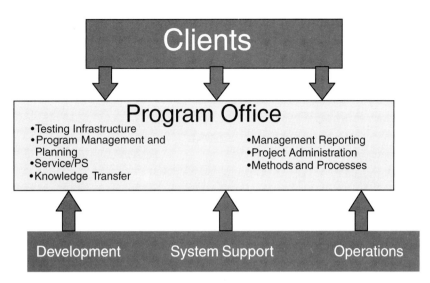

Figure 10–1 Program office plan

both sides comprise the program office. The purpose of the program office is to have mutually agreed-upon deliverables, standards in communication, business processes, rollout plans that match both sides, and a coordination framework among other vendors (like Ariba and Oracle) and the internal development teams. Figure 10–1 illustrates the program office plan.

▶ Project Management Approach

The PM's fundamental activities are to plan, structure, control, and lead. This is true for projects of all kinds and applies whether the PM is managing an e-business project, a bunch of e-business projects constituting a program, or even a business process. Here, the approach is rapid iterative and release- and deliverable-based. We will explain these in more detail later.

Project Plan

Figure 10–2 shows a very high-level plan that maps the initial activities. The plan is developed as the project proceeds.

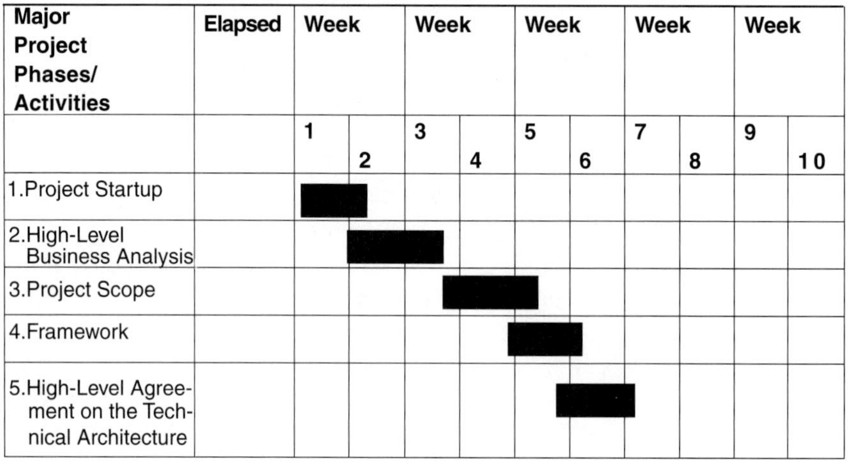

Major Project Phases/ Activities	Elapsed	Week		Week		Week		Week		Week	
		1	2	3	4	5	6	7	8	9	10
1.Project Startup		██									
2.High-Level Business Analysis			██								
3.Project Scope				██							
4.Framework						██					
5.High-Level Agreement on the Technical Architecture							██				

Figure 10–2   Plan for initial activities

Coordinating the project

In the coordination activity, several things are done. First, the initial team is created, and then it is expanded into the program office. The different groups are identified, for example, the Ariba PM, Oracle PM, IT PMs, etc. A communication plan is generated. Executive sponsors are lined up on all sides.

Forming the e-business project team

Vendor S proposes to conduct this assignment using a team of consultants, systems engineers, professional service staff, and a program manager. The program manager is the single point of contact for ABC and the coordinator for all activities. The Vendor S team is shown in Table 10–1. The team will be extended later.

Table 10–1   Vendor S Project Team

Title	Team Member Name
Program Manager	
E-Business PM	
Consultants/System Engineers	
Professional Services	

Assigning roles and responsibilities

Vendor S's approach to staffing this e-business project requires the use of experienced professionals, well-versed in IT planning and implementation.

Team members' responsibilities are as follows:

- **Program manager**—The program manager is the point person to manage the e-business program. This person, together with the PMs, will review the quality of the deliverables at each milestone to ensure that the work meets Vendor S's professional standards.

- **E-business PM**—The PM will be responsible for meeting ABC's expectation on deliverables. The PM will serve as the focal point for day-to-day contact between ABC's PM and Vendor S, and will often serve as an advisor to the ABC PM throughout the implementation and transition efforts. The PM will lead the e-business project through the whole program.

- **Consultants and systems engineers**—These are experienced practitioners who are skilled in technical aspects of the products. They provide guidance to the Vendor S team and e-business project team and participate in all activities of the implementation phase.

- **Professional service staff**—This service is available from Vendor S if ABC wants some billable consulting and development help.

E-Business Project Team Organization, Roles, and Responsibilities

This e-business project is organized to encourage participation of a combined ABC/Vendor S team to expedite a smooth bidirectional osmosis of knowledge and get support from the executive sponsors. Following is an overview of the project's structure (also see Figure 10–3).

- **Executive and steering committees**—The current senior executive committees will serve as sponsors for the e-business project. These committees will ensure that their staff fully comprehends the project's priority and allocate resources required for success-

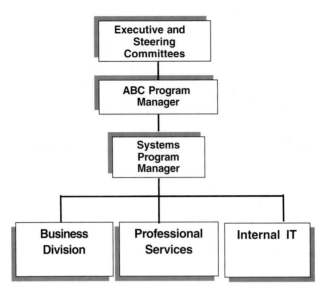

Figure 10–3   E-business project team's organization, roles, and responsibilities

ful implementation. As ultimate decision-makers, they will be visible and maintain meaningful participation in the implementation effort.

- **ABC program manager**—The Vendor S program manager will work closely with the ABC program manager. They will be responsible for resolving any issues. Their roles are critical in communicating and supporting the overall implementation process.

Communication

To ensure the overall success of the implementation, the Vendor S program manager produces formal weekly status reports for ABC. These reports provide information concerning the status and progress of the e-business project by identifying and addressing the following items:

- E-business project team's accomplishments for the reporting period
- Objectives for the next period

- Key issues that may affect the overall success of the e-business project
- Action items requiring immediate attention
- Outlook to completion according to the e-business project plan
- Reviews conducted at major milestone points during the e-business project

Communication is done via email, face-to-face meetings, Web postings, and sometimes Web-enabled meetings.

Continuous Transition Approach

At a summary level, Vendor S's approach for transition is driven by an assessment of skills. The training and communications plan is results-based and relies on the following disciplines:

- **Knowledge transfer**—It is Vendor S's practice to conduct training sessions in the beginning and throughout the engagement process to ensure that all the team members, including the executive sponsors, understand the e-commerce process. Vendor S will pair experienced Vendor S consultants and client staff to work on all activities. Vendor S will educate ABC on the hardware, software, and procedures to meet its desired goal of more self-sufficiency in those areas. Vendor S uses both structured and unstructured training methods to accomplish a rapid knowledge transfer. Vendor S also believes in a train the trainer approach for rapid dissemination of knowledge.
- **Team-driven**—An e-business project team consists of representatives from different disciplines and organizational units. This approach, through the extensive use of on-the-job training, individualized sessions, and formal training events, promotes cooperative, educational, and cross-functional relationships among the team members.
- **Results- and implementation-oriented**—While a well-thought-out process is critical to the success of an implementation, the Vendor S implementation focuses on results. The training effort ties directly to the exact needs of ABC. The measure of a successful e-business project is not the completion of the installa-

tion only, but the ease with which the new infrastructure is adopted by the ABC staff after the implementation.

- **Use of automated tools**—Vendor S's training includes an integrated set of techniques and tools (videos, computer-based training (CBT), and Internet–based training) to facilitate the learning process.

Project Control

The e-business project scope is continually being worked on. Initially, only one division and one type of product are chosen as part of the use case analysis. Functionality like cataloguing, quick-deliver mechanisms, and Web-enabled EDI is being discussed, and a high-level requirements analysis is being done. Ariba's punchout capability for cataloguing is a critical piece of this implementation.

Critical Success Factors

The critical success factors for a timely implementation of this e-business project are as follows:

- Demonstrated executive support and sponsorship
- Team availability and commitment
- Cooperation from ABC's business and corporate IS organization
- Frequent, effective communication among the e-business PMs

E-Business Project Management Tools

To manage complex e-projects, appropriate tools are needed. There are many e-project management tools on the market. Only a few important ones will be discussed.

Effective project management is not just planning, delivering, and tracking—it is collaboration and communication, also. Team play allows two-way communications between PM and project team. It is also fully Web-enabled and allows Web-based collaboration, which is essential in e-business project management.

There are several e-business project management software tools like:

- E-project Executive by Critical Path Technical Services, Inc.
- E-project Exchange by IMS Information Management Services, Inc.
- Action Plan by Netmosphere, Inc.
- E-project Office by Pacific Edge Software, Inc.
- Program management solutions from Robbins-Giola, Inc.
- Project/process management software (Architect) from James Martin and Co., etc.

Some of these tools are very extensive, integrate different methodologies, and handle business-oriented projects to very technical projects. The important point here is to find the right tool for the project. Web collaboration and communication are very important for the e-business environment and project/program handling. Also, most e-business programs consist of multiple projects. E-tools need to handle this complexity and the interdependencies of tasks between projects.

The following Web sites contain extensive materials on project management disciplines, tools, processes, and articles:

- http://www.pmforum.org/prof/apma.htm
- http://www.sdmagazine.com/

▶ Business Elements

These tasks are needed to understand the business needs of a company—an e-business or a traditional organization that is moving in the direction of an e-business. The elements cited below are some examples (not an exhaustive list) of e-business elements:

- **Business modeling**—Using various methodologies and facilitated sessions, e-business markets, e-strategies, and e-positioning are clearly modeled. This understanding of the e-business models is extremely important for large e-business initiatives. Even for smaller, more tactical e-business projects, an understanding of the business issues to some depth helps align projects with e-business directions. Most consulting companies have their own methodologies.

There are, of course, different levels of business modeling—in our case, it is done in the context of a strategic level. In applications design and analysis, people do business modeling at a more specific level to analyze a particular business context, for example, doing business modeling of an inventory control system with parts and suppliers.

- **Financial modeling**—Analyzes an e-business' financial situation, including its financial ratios. This can be part of a business model. The reason why we mention this type of modeling separately is that, depending on the e-initiative, this could even be a very specific, tactical ROI analysis without explicit links to the business model. Some sample questions and templates to capture business information from a business unit and IT are contained in Table 10–2.

Table 10–2   Questions to Capture Business Information

Questions	
General Information	
Vision and Mission of the Company	
Market Information	• What is the market share of the main products? • What is the growth rate of the company? • Any analysis on the experts of the • company? • What are the markets this company is going after?
Financials	• What is the annual revenue of the company? • What is the net income? • What is the growth rate for both figures above? • Inventory turns? • Cash flows? • Debts? • Earnings per Share (EPS)? • Any other financial information that may be deemed necessary:

Table 10–2 Questions to Capture Business Information (Continued)

Organization	• What are the different divisions and their heads? • Geographic location of each division? • Budget of each division? • What are the major reorganizations/re-engineering efforts going on? • What are the major projects/product developments going on? • What are the bottlenecks in various business processes?

- **Cultural analysis**—Analyzes the culture of a customer. This can be part of a business model, also. Cultural analysis is primarily a people-related element. However, it is also linked with the business processes and future goals of the e-business and it is worth treating it as a business element, also.

- **Competitive analysis**—Analyzes the client's competitors. This is definitely an integral part of the development of an e-business model.

- **Organizational modeling**—Analyzes the organizational structure of customers, their politics, and spheres of influence; looks at whether the organizational structure can sustain its business. In organizational modeling, the as-is organizational structure is examined and a to-be structure that will sustain the new e-business models is built.

- **Enterprise-wide business/technology analysis**—This is a series of workshops and interviews to analyze the business needs and the technology that will support them.

  It is a picture of high-level analysis—detailed analysis, interviews, workshops—then deliverables.

- **Architectural overview**—This is a current assessment of the client's business architecture and provides high-level recommendations. The goal of most e-business initiatives is to change existing business architectures to new ones.

- **Strategic planning**—Strategic planning is like a thread that ties all the different business elements together. For large-scale e-business and e-commerce initiatives, a strategic planning process is a must.

- **IT planning**—Plan with IT staff to see how all the IT e-initiatives are in sync with each other and with the e-business goals set by the company. A lot of this can be done using value chain analysis and value chain linking.

▶ People Elements

People elements are often the most neglected in e-business projects. However, they are very important. Any business starts with customers and ends with customers. So, customer-facing, effective business processes with properly motivated, skilled people communicating effectively with one another are critical elements in e-business projects. A process is as good as the people enabling the process. The following are some examples:

- Skills development
- Roles and responsibilities
- Cultural analysis
- Communication styles
- Training
- Mentoring
- Job descriptions
- Performance evaluation
- Staffing
- People analysis
- HR programs

The above set of people elements are just examples of people elements that any e-business initiative has to understand and focus on.

Skills Development

Most e-business initiatives are about change—drastic change. Change in thought, change in processes, change in the ways of business, and change in the use of technology. One of the first things that needs to be seriously evaluated is the skill set of the "to-be" world vs. the "as-is" world. This gap analysis of skill sets will lead to a path of learning for individuals and eventually to the e-organization as a whole. There are various skills development techniques, but the shift of an e-organization's learning almost always follows the following curve (Figure 10–4). The exact nature of the steps depends on the culture, existing knowledge, and technology base.

As an organization moves or adopts new paradigms, the skill sets needed obviously change. The new ways of work demand new skill sets. However, the retooling and relearning need to happen in a planned process. New behaviors, new work processes, and ethics need to be envisioned and ultimately institutionalized.

Roles and Responsibilities

This is an e-business project management task, but it is also a people task or element. Clear roles and responsibilities are important not only in an e-business project context, but also within an organiza-

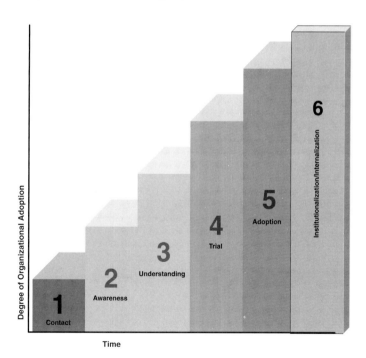

Figure 10–4   Organizational change adoption

tional context. The creation of an organizational chart is to clearly state who does what. In an e-business initiative, understanding the roles, responsibilities, and organizational structure is a critical success factor. This is mainly because most e-business initiatives cut across the organization. The sphere of influence of each person and organizational structure, the politics, and the implicit and explicit roles of people are important contributors to the success of an e-business initiative.

Cultural Analysis

Most e-initiatives end up directly affecting the culture of a company. The speed of traditional methods is inadequate. The 4D Framework specifically emphasizes organizational culture as part of change management, value chain analysis, and the value chain linking process. We have kept the cultural analysis very simple so it can be captured in a template and then used as a baseline for the as-is organizational culture (Table 10–3). We may then decide on a to-be organizational culture and design a change management program to change the culture for the e-business initiatives to realize their full value (as determined in value chain analysis and linking).

Table 10–3 As-Is and To-Be Cultural Analysis

Culture Category	Score = Green/Yellow/Red
Cost-effective	
Service-focused	
Innovative (product and service)	
Technology-focused	
Business-focused	
Process-focused	
Team-oriented	
Decision-making speed	
Implementation speed	

Communication Styles

Different communication styles relate to different types of people. One of the important aspects of managing e-initiatives is to understand the different types of people and their communications styles and manage them accordingly. We briefly mention one of the social style theories. Teams can be divided into four groups of people:

- Analytical
- Driver
- Amiable
- Expressive

The job of the e-business PM is to be versatile and use different management and communication styles when dealing with different types of people.

- **Training**—Training and education to develop knowledge and skill sets are important components in any e-business initiative. The details of training will not be dealt with here. Training is a very important part of change management.

- **Mentoring**—This is part of training and quickens the development of people. A mentor shares his or her experience with the person being mentored and guides him/her through real-world scenarios.

- **Job descriptions**—This is again a people element and an important part of hiring and retaining people. Creating a very succinct and clear job description is not a trivial task. Most successful e-business studies show that choosing the right people was the most important task.

- **Performance evaluation**—This is a subject by itself. However, due to the challenging nature of e-business initiatives and scarcity of talented people to be part of the e-commerce movement, it becomes essential to do proper performance evaluation to reward the right people.

- **Staffing**—One of the most difficult tasks (elements) is hiring the right person for the right job. The details of hiring are outside the scope of this book.

- **People analysis**—There are many different people analysis theories—Briggs Meyers is a well-known method. E-business initiatives often tend to ignore some of these basic people elements, which may lead to failure.
- **HR programs**—Programs that emphasize people and human resources—incentive schemes, commissions and bonuses, the overall benefits program of any company, stock options tied to performance—all have profound effects on the success of e-business initiatives. HR-related software is quite popular. Peoplesoft is one of the leading HR software tools.

▶ Technology Elements

The list below contains some technology-related (application/data/hardware and management) tasks. This task list should undergo modification in the future as it is put into practice.

Implementation Planning	System Installation
Transition/Migration Planning	Software Installation
Knowledge Transfer	System Configuration Planning
Storage Planning	
Software Change Management	Site Certification
Capacity Planning Process	Operational Skills Analysis
Benchmarking	
Systems Analysis/Design	Technical Training
Data Frameworks/Architectures	Backup Procedure
Network Frameworks/Architectures	Fault Management
Data Flow Diagrams (DFDs)	IT Disaster Recovery/Best Practices
Object-Oriented Programming (OOP)	Infrastructure Management Planning
Rapid Application Development (RAD)	Buy/Build/Component Assembly Process
Buy/Build/Assemble	
Technical Architectures	Software Design Methodologies
Prototyping	
Data Center Management Issues (Best-of-Breed)	
IT Management Issues	
Vendor/Package Selection	
Use Analysis	
IPE	

- **Implementation planning**—Creates an implementation plan for a solution. It will incorporate installation phases and other related phases and tasks.

- **Transition/migration planning**—Will also handle the soft issues of migration and change management issues.

- **Knowledge transfer**—Essentially, this represents a plan to transfer knowledge to different parts of an organization. It takes into account a total approach to training and education. A big part of this was discussed in the change management chapter.

- **Software change management**—This issue comes up whenever a new patch or new version of software is going to be implemented. Software change management is a process that ensures that the impact of software changes is minimal on the new environment.

- **Capacity planning process**—This is a process to evaluate the capacity needs of a certain environment and make recommendations. For most e-businesses, annual/semi-annual capacity planning processes do not work anymore. IT organizations are moving toward a continuous capacity planning process and vendors have started providing this with pay per usage types of concepts.

- **Benchmarking**—Benchmarking is a process to evaluate some measurement parameters and compare them against some standard matrix. Hardware performance, database performance, etc. are measured.

- **System analysis/design**—This procedure analyzes application system requirements and designs the system. As discussed earlier, the waterfall method is obsolete for Web-based application development. A very fast, iterative method is preferred.

- **Data frameworks**—These represent Entity Relationship (ER) type frameworks for data relationships and database designs.

- **Network/system architectures**—Design networks to provide infrastructure solutions. An example of a high-level system architecture is shown in Figure 10–5.

- **Data flow diagrams**—DFDs are used to design applications. Figure 10–6 is basically a DFD that analyzes a customer order and its relationships to other important entities. Though traditionalists believe in DFDs, in e-commerce projects, more

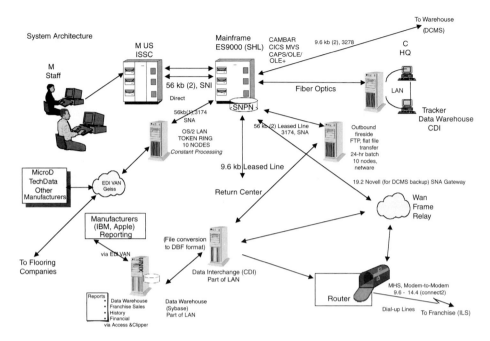

Figure 10–5   High-level system architecture diagram

emphasis is given to object-oriented (OO) methodologies, design techniques, and tools.

- **Object-oriented programming/design**—An advanced design methodology, OO is an integral part of e-commerce development. The basic OO concept is that an engineering approach can be used in software development. Electronic products can be made out of chips, similarly, software applications can be constructed out of pre-fabricated software "chips," or objects.

OO development is also known as *component-based development*. The component-based method is service-driven—each layer in the architecture offers *services* to higher layers but hides the details of how those services are implemented. Software components at a certain level of abstraction were always part of structured design, but traditionally, they have been like application programming interfaces (APIs) and system-level calls.

Application components are at a much higher business level and offer services that address business logic and functionality. Components provide business-centric services and hide the

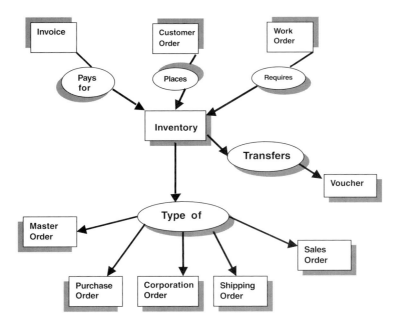

Figure 10–6   Data flow diagrams

details of technology involved. This will allow applications programmers, systems analysts and architects to concentrate more on business issues rather than the details of technology.

Finger, Kumar, and Sharma, in their book *Enterprise E-Commerce*, divide e-commerce application components into three main categories:

- Cross-application components
- Application-specific components
- Industry-specific components[1]

The services provided by cross-application components can be consumed across few applications. The granularity of the components is somewhat higher than device driver level but lower than that provided by application-specific components.

1.   Finger, Peter, Harsha Kumar, and Tarun Sharma, *Enterprise E-Commerce* (Tampa, FL: Meghan-Kiffer Press, 2000).

Application-specific components provide a higher level of granularity than cross-application components and often use these components to provide application-specific functionality.

An industry-specific component is vertical market specific. Usually an industry-specific component will consume the services of application-specific component, and an application-specific component will consume the cross-applications components.

- **Build/buy/assemble**—The following summarizes the advantages/disadvantages of these three approaches. The assemble approach is the preferable approach in many e-commerce application development projects.

  In the build approach, the application is developed from scratch and goes through the typical system development cycle. Very detailed knowledge is needed at various levels. A build approach is normally very technology-oriented and the application developed can cater to the business requirements. However, implementation is very resource-intensive and often prolonged. Changes in business requirements can be reflected in the application, but they are time- and cost-intensive.

  In the buy approach, the application is bought and some modifications are done. Often, the application does not align with the business logic and so either the enterprise needs to change the business logic or the package needs to be changed. The buy approach has yielded mixed results and some packages have a very high total cost of ownership (TCO), especially because of long and complex implementation cycles.

  The component assembly approach seems to allow a greater focus on business logic and less emphasis on the code development details. Well-developed components can enhance systems development time and build a flexible systems development environment.

- **Rapid application development**—This is an application development method intended to roll out application development faster. The fundamental philosophy is to take a small subset of business problems, develop applications very interactively with the user community using RAD tools, and deliver solutions. Applications, therefore, are delivered in an iterative and interactive manner. Most e-commerce development tools are RAD-based.

RAD as a methodology has been around for a while. In the context of e-business, RAD is very closely coupled with component-based development.

- **Technology architectures**—These help in understanding an application at various tiers. Figure 10–7 is an example of technology architectures.

- **Prototyping**—Several different types of prototyping exist, including hardware and software prototyping. Prototyping can be used in an organizational context also, which is called organizational prototyping. In e-commerce development, prototyping is a very integral part of the overall development process.

- **Data center management**—Tasks will help issues surrounding the data center. Backup procedures, disaster recovery, data center layouts, and so on fall in this category.

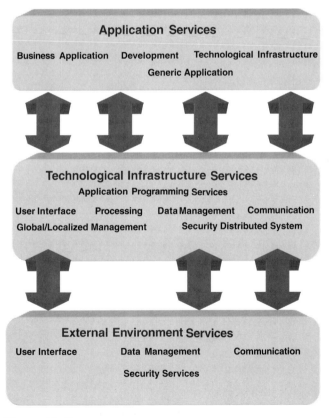

Figure 10–7   Technology architecture

- **IT management**—Tasks ensure that the e-business project team understands the IT management issues—different frameworks of IT organizations, IT budgeting process, IT culture, IT deadlines, etc.
- **Vendor (package) selection**—This task ensures that clients are comfortable with the system packages (e.g., SAP/Baan/Oracle/Peoplesoft). Figure 10–8 illustrates a process to select a vendor.

System installation, software installation, system configuration planning, storage planning, site certification, operational skills analysis, training (technical), backup procedures, fault management, IT disaster

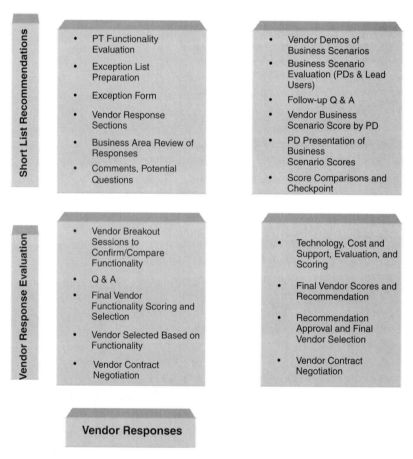

Figure 10–8   Vendor selection process

recovery best practices, and many other technical elements are better articulated in other, more relevant literature.

The original decision for ABC to choose vendors like Ariba and Commerce One was changed and a component-based assembly approach was taken instead. This was done during the buy vs. assemble analysis and the team voted in favor of an assembly approach. The team used the 4D Framework, started evaluating all the elements simultaneously, and kicked off teams to look into hardware and networking needs in parallel. The team also engaged cross-company initiatives for handing policy changes and procedures and instituted the communication and training associated with those changes. In short, the team took a flexible framework like the 4D Framework and used some of its very important elements and principles to successfully implement this e-business initiative.

The 4D Framework was applied in the following way:

In the understanding phase, the team did a process redesign that resulted in an organizational change of multiple procurement divisions to one consolidated procurement business process reporting to one vice president of procurement. In the context of e-business, this had to be done rapidly. So, an HVPM approach was invoked in the current analysis step to look at the current procurement processes, compare them with available best practices in the industry, and then proceed to an e-procurement process redesign step. The template shown in Figure 10–9 was one of the process evaluation checklists used.

Process Assessment Evaluation Checklist

During the presentation of the new design process, some of the items in this list were addressed. The overall assessment was a go with no major changes required (based on the feedback received from the relevant managers).

During the process redesign step and afterward, the team started evaluating enabling technologies in what is called technology-enabled visioning. It was at this time that the team did a buy/build/assemble decision-making process and agreed to do a component-based assembly. The case study here focused more on the development side. The HVPM chapter (Chapter 7) dealt with more examples on the e-business process side.

	Validation Criteria	Comments	
	New Design	Yes	No
1.	Are we addressing the right problem?		
2.	Does the new (modified) design solve the problem as you see it?		
3.	Were all root causes addressed?		
4.	Are all key events present and appropriate?		
5.	Are all the key participants present and appropriate?		
6.	Is the proposed solution manageable?		
	Performance Criteria		
1.	Are they present and measurable?		
2.	Are they tracking/measuring the right things?		
	Implementation		
1.	Is the plan adequate and feasible?		
2.	Are key costs identified and reasonable?		
3.	Are key benefits identified and reasonable?		
4.	If there are some risky elements, are they clearly identified and contained?		
5.	Is there a backup plan if the new design cannot be implemented as planned?		
6.	Is there a process manager identified, if necessary?		
7.	Is there a criteria to measure the success of the process manager?		

Figure 10–9 Validation criteria assessment process

	Validation Criteria	Comments	
	Issues and Recommendations	Yes	No
1.	Are there showstoppers?		
2.	Do you agree with the overall recommendations?		
	Report Format and Clarity		
1.	Is the report ready to be published?		
	Overall Assessment	Initial	
1.	_____ Go, no additional changes required.		
2.	_____ Go, with minor corrections.		
3.	_____ No go, changes needed.		
4.	_____ No go, major revisions required.		

Figure 10–9   Validation criteria assessment process (Continued)

▶ Process Elements

The following is a list of process elements. Again, process elements overlap with all the other elements and even the e-business project management functions. This is not an exhaustive list of process elements—only a few have been listed, and even fewer important ones discussed in more detail:

- Change management
- Value chain linking process
- Application development process
- Business case analysis process
- Business processes (HR-related)
- Transition management process
- Production Quality Analysis (QA)/Acceptance Process
- Problem Management
- IT change management

- Internal support agreement/process
- Event monitoring
- Performance management and capacity planning
- Software change management
- Capacity planning process
- Disaster recovery process
- Asset management
- Systems and infrastructure management
- Charge-back process
- IT planning process
- E-business project planning process

As discussed earlier, process elements touch all other elements. We will discuss some of the important processes here and some more later.

Change Management

Change management is a very critical process that deserves separate treatment. Change management is also one of the foundations of the 4D Framework.

The value chain linking process, which is discussed in a separate chapter, is also a foundation discipline that touches other elements of the 4D Framework. It basically links desired results to e-initiatives.

Business Case Analysis Process

Organizations follow a business case analysis process to find out whether the e-business or e-commerce project is viable and makes sense. Often, targeted goals are linked with the e-initiatives to see if the linkage and contribution are strong enough to make a proper financial and business case to pursue the e-initiatives.

Business Processes (HR-Related)

Figure 10–10 shows an HR business process. The following are some very important business processes in any e-organization:

- E-procurement business process
- E-order business process
- E-marketing business process, and more

BPR was popularized by Michael Hammer and James Champy, two management consultants. The fundamental emphasis of this philosophy was to reorganize organizations around business processes and not functional divisions. This theoretically would reduce handoffs and delays and produce efficient business processes, which would focus on a particular business process from start to finish and not just part of the process. So, for example, an ordering business process would have order entry, credit verification, billing, accounting, and logistics tightly linked together with less than one process manager rather than five different divisions with five different division heads. Technology is an enabler. A typical application development environment that supports any business process is shown in Figure 10–11.

The success of BPR in its totality was mixed. The initial hype blew the whole thing out of proportion. Also, it ignored the human side of any organization. Additionally, it underestimated the cost of change and the complex issues of change. BPR's mixed success led us in our 4D Framework to emphasize the importance of change management as well as the human aspects of any change. E-business initiatives have a very similar impact—that is, they often challenge the functional areas of organizations to work together.

Figure 10–12 shows how business processes are often a combination of functional areas. E-business processes help in breaking down functional silos and reduce the handoffs between functional areas.

Hiring Process for New Employees

Human resource manager establishes the need for new employees.

Validates against approved budget.

Online requisition is routed to Compensation Department.

Notify, pending review by Compensation Department.

Recruiting Department

The Compensation Department will notify the HR manager and Recruiting Department of an approval or rejection.

It's then forwarded to the Recruiting Department.

The search process begins, supported by an online applicant tracking system; post job, internally, if required (provide online capability).

Applicant is identified; interview(s) is scheduled via phone, letter, etc.

Offer Extended to Candidate

If offer is rejected:

The applicant's information is kept for future access.
The requisition is reactivated.
The search begins once again.

If the candidate accepts offer:

Job offer process is initiated.
Hiring process is initiated.
Online notifications to Benefits and Security Departments.
If relocating, route details to Relocation Services, online.
Update organization chart.

Benefits Enrollment Generated

Online eligibility for benefits enrollment is performed; benefits package is generated, online; package to employees.

Benefits package returned by new employee.

Online notification to insurance carriers.

Online notification to payroll.

Update system for eligibility of benefits.

Online notification to employee confirming benefits.

Paper document confirming benefits sent to employee's home.

Figure 10–10   HR Business process flow

Application Development Environment

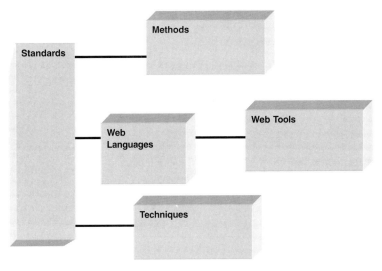

Figure 10–11   Application development process for e-business

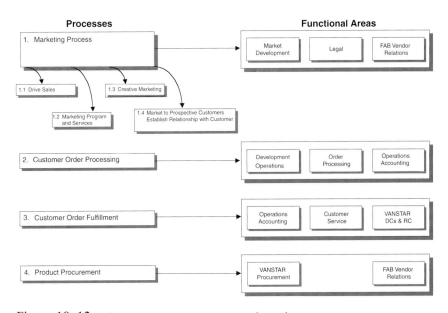

Figure 10–12   Business process re-engineering

Transition Management Process

Transition Management Process provides a path to e-transition. Figure 10–13 gives a comprehensive view of how a traditional company can transition into an e-business.

Transition strategy considers all the aspects of an organization such as business, people, process, and technology and aligns them to realize beneficial targets. (See Table 10–4.)

Table 10–4   Transition Management Process

Radical Changes and Improvements	• Updated manuals • Online access by customers • More modifications treated during the cycle • Revisions in different manuals are in-line • More modifications treated during the cycle

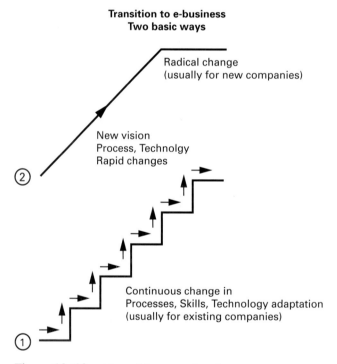

Figure 10–13   Transition to e-business

Table 10–4   Transition Management Process (Continued)

Incremental Changes and Improvements	• Continuous flow processing • Workflow management • Program management • Concurrent writing/editing • Reduce delays • Group activities • Eliminate controls

Production QA/Acceptance Process

Production acceptance (PA) complements application development, ensuring that sufficient operational requirements and considerations are accounted for in the architecture, design, development, and deployment of new systems. This process also ensures that new and changing systems are identified and operational requirements are prepared for and met on schedule—not at the last minute.

The PA process is a critical piece of any distributed computing infrastructure. PA helps set the stage to provide the same level of reliability, availability, and serviceability to the new distributed environment as did the legacy infrastructure.

The PA process is composed of two phases: deployment and ongoing operations. For each phase, operational requirements are identified within each support function and managed through readiness.

The PA process provides requirements to appropriate operations staff to prepare them to support new e-initiatives. In essence, this process acts as the glue among users, development, and support organizations. The process of identifying an application's support requirements develops, or at the very least, contributes to an IT operation's support level agreements for the application being deployed. It establishes the vehicle required to effectively communicate with all other groups, developers, and users.

Problem Management

A centralized process is needed to manage and resolve user network, application, and system problems.

The purpose of problem management is to establish an ongoing process of resolving problems, minimizing the impact affecting IT services and optimizing the time and effort spent in resolution. The problem management process facilitates immediate resolution, without wasting time to figure out how to manage a problem. This is achieved by setting into motion a management process that encompasses an "interdepartmental" problem effort that will effectively manage the measurements of a tracking, escalation, resolution, and reporting system.

Problem management is composed of many parts. One of these parts is the problem control mechanism, which has as its objective the resolution of problems in a data processing environment. As you will see, the scope of problem management is not limited to the help desk, but also applies to all IS functions and processes.

Four key areas of problem management include:

- **Measurement**—When a data processing system fails to operate as planned, the problem management system is the first place where a recorded indication of that failure is made. No other operational system has the responsibility of recording failure occurrence for all failures. Thus, the problem management system has the responsibility to obtain a complete and accurate account of the problem to assist in the management decision process. This also means creating the ability to measure levels of service, including response, resolution, open issues, and exceptions.

- **Tracking/escalation**—A tracking function is performed to assure that all problems are addressed appropriately. If some of those problems breach the guidelines established by management for resolution time or an action plan, they are escalated as required. This means that it is always a management decision to allow a problem to remain in an exception status. It also means that this decision will be reviewed on a regular basis until the problem is resolved or is no longer in exception status.

- **Control**—The problem management system utilizes control in several ways. The first is through procedures that are established to dictate the way in which problems are logged and processed by the system. A second form of control is in the early identification of problems through trend analysis. This control function can detect and escalate problems before they have major system impact. Finally, control is established through the specific assignment of responsibilities for problem activities.

- **Reporting**—The final contribution of the problem management system is to provide information to management to allow them to control the system. Without accurate and timely information, management will not be able to make proper decisions to control the problem. This reporting mechanism also contributes to performance metrics, allowing management to set and monitor measurements.

IT Change Management

This process coordinates any change that can potentially affect the operational production environment.

Change management is a very simple concept. Just as processes, such as version release management are actual methods of changing and maintaining the release of objects between the test and the production environments, the change management process provides an orderly way to go about managing changes. It means notifying those affected by the change beforehand, and listening to protest should the change have adverse effects. It means documenting changes and devising reasonable contingency plans for restoring the system if a change doesn't work.

A change is any addition or modification to a data processing system that could potentially affect the stability of the production environment. Areas of change include, but are not limited to, hardware, system software (operating system), application software, networks, the environment (heating, cooling, and so on), and documentation.

When implementing change management, the fatal flaw in distributed systems is not that they don't have enough controls and practices, but that there are not good checks and balances to detect unauthorized changes or unforeseen consequences. Checks and balances processes, especially for change control, help eliminate human error, improve the efficiency and effectiveness of the process, and ensure the maintenance of systems availability.

Asset Management

This process includes efficient discovery, storage, tracking, querying, and end-of-life processes of open enterprise computing resources, including hardware, operating systems, and applications.

The processes for asset management require the owner of the resources to define the assets to be managed. From there, an assessment is made on what data exists to match that definition and what tools will be used to manage it. Once tools are in place, defined data is entered. Assets being managed require an end-of-life process. Requirements for this process will be determined and implemented by the asset management owner.

Changes and updates to the production environment are tracked by the change management system. Changes to non-production elements defined as assets to be tracked, such as desktop units, will need to be updated in a more manual fashion.

Event Monitoring

This is a process that monitors specified events in the environment, including status and unforeseen incidents on the network, within databases, and/or with applications. The process and supporting tools monitor predetermined events (i.e., transfers, faults, thresholds, etc.), give proactive status or alerts, and escalate them appropriately.

Event monitoring is a core component in the data center environment to other related processes such as performance monitoring/capacity planning. It provides the interface and input to data required by these processes.

The event monitoring process utilizes the network management system to interface with the console management, performance monitoring/capacity planning, asset management, and problem management processes to form a display and control layer. This display and control layer will provide operations with problems, events, and outstanding requests, and will capture alerts from console and event monitoring tools, which in turn provide and/or feed information to other management and monitoring systems (i.e., problem management).

Performance Management and Capacity Planning

These provide a global view of network and system resource utilization, which identifies potential performance problems and provides sufficient computing resources to support current and future business requirements.

These two subjects should be quite familiar to mainframe-based data centers as components of an ongoing difficult problem: How many computing resources do you need, and when do you need them? Distributed client/server environments must also wrestle with this problem, plus they have the added complexity of dealing with multiple sites, not just one central computer room.

By supporting the functions of capacity planning and performance monitoring, IT organizations are really assessing the service levels they are providing. The service levels are driven by customer expectations:

- What service will be provided?
- What service can a given configuration provide?

Difficulties with this arise for several reasons:

- Customers are not always forthcoming about their expected usage patterns, and they "always" find new ways of using "all" the computing resources available.
- The rate of change in new technologies is rapid and continuing to accelerate.
- The infrastructures of the hardware and software components of a given environment are now so complex that you are often dealing with technical specialists (experts in one component are rarely experts in another).

In the e-business world, capacity planning is a continuous process—fixed time planning does not work since the business demand trends have totally changed from the past. So, the focus has been to do continuous planning. The infrastructure vendors' business model has changed because of that. Vendors are now creating a pay per usage model; for instance, if you use four processors now and six tomorrow, you will be charged according to the usage.

Internal Support Agreement/Process

There are no structured agreements between the different functional areas within IT. Expectations are not clearly defined, leading to communication and relationship problems between infrastructure support and other IT functional areas. A critical problem is the lack of communication between the application development and production support areas.

Without internal support agreements, it is difficult to implement and support business-critical applications and ensure quality and high levels of availability. Without well-defined responsibilities, expectations, and procedures, coordination between the applications development and infrastructure support areas will be affected, resulting in a negative impact on IT's ability to avoid and resolve problems.

As IT continues to grow, it is critical that an internal support agreement be designed and implemented between the IT infrastructure support functions and the other IT functions, especially applications development.

IT Customer Satisfaction Process

IT cannot function in a vacuum. Knowing your customer's level of satisfaction with the systems and services you provide is an integral part of the overall IT management charter.

In the past, measuring customer satisfaction has always been a bureaucratic and ineffective process. Sending out quarterly survey forms and pleading with customers to fill them out was truly a waste of time and effort. IT was lucky to get a 30% return rate. IT needs to capture 100% response from all customers. The process needs to be in real time, not survey a week/month later.

A process to measure internal customer satisfaction for all services that IT provides and every trouble ticket or work request serviced by IT should be implemented.

It is also suggested that IT develop a process to track and measure all services provided to its online customers by capturing information about their "online experience."

Disaster Recovery

A well-planned, contingent system to enable (business-defined) recovery in the event of a disaster should be in place. Murphy's Law is never more appropriate than when applied to computers. That is why smart businesses invest wisely in disaster recovery programs.

Lack of a well-planned, continuously updated, and tested disaster recovery plan can lead to disaster. Remember the rule: If you have a good disaster recovery plan, you may never need to use it to its full extent. However, if you do not have a good disaster recovery plan, you will invariably wish you did when disaster strikes.

The purpose of this contingency plan is to provide for the recovery of the mission-critical business processing performed on production servers in the data center in case of the loss of this processing capability due to an unforeseen incident. The recovery goal is to recover any mission-critical processing capability within a predefined timeframe from the time a disaster is declared.

A key to the disaster recovery model is a production recovery facility (PRF). This quite simply is the location and environment in which mission-critical business processing will be restored in the event of an emergency.

Configuration Management/Release Distribution

After change management is defined, the release distribution and configuration management processes are the actual methods used to change and maintain a release of objects (hardware, system software, application software, etc.) between the staging and the production environments.

Software Change Management

Data centers of old had very rigorous software patch and change management processes. In the UNIX world also, version control is well-established. In the Web world, version control and patch releases are often done in a microscopic form and moved out over the Web just in time. However, the Web software change control process is still developing. Software releases over the Web are also becoming very frequent; that is, small software changes are made and released to users over the Web.

AOL uses this JIT software release approach.

Systems and Infrastructure Management

These are processes to manage applications, system software, databases, networks, telecommunication equipment, and system infrastructure. In the e-business context, remote management of infrastructure is extremely important—so is the management of mainframe-type infrastructures, along with UNIX boxes, PCs, and thin clients (like Sun Rays, etc.). In traditional data centers, system management disciplines are well-established. Mainframe processes and system management tools are very mature. In open systems (e.g., UNIX) and e-commerce applications, the systems management tools and processes are still not mature enough to handle today's more complex computing environments. However, e-businesses need to have well-thought-out processes and system management tools to handle the increased volume and complexity.

Charge-Back Process

This is an enterprise-wide process to charge back to the business units the IT software and hardware usage via some internal charges that will keep track of each division's actual usage vs. the budget allocated.

IT Planning Process

An IT planning process is linked with the business planning process and lays out the vision, mission, and objective of the IT division. It then shows the different current initiatives, and future initiatives, and deals with the budgets and actual expenses. This again is becoming a very iterative and continuous process in an e-business context.

Case Study

Here we will use company ABC again and give a scenario of an e-business solution from business redesign to the actual deployment of technology using some of the elements/tasks/methodologies discussed in the 4D Framework. The previous case study dealt with the project/program management aspects; here, application development is emphasized. Also, the original decision of ABC to choose vendors like Ariba and Commerce One was changed and a component-based assembly approach was taken. This was done via some business case analysis of buy vs. assemble and the team voted in favor of an assembly approach. The team used the 4D Framework, started evaluating all the elements simultaneously, and kicked off teams to look into hardware and networking needs in parallel. The team also engaged cross-company initiatives for handing policy changes and procedures, as well as the communication and training associated with those changes. In short, the team took a flexible framework like the 4D Framework and used some of its important elements and principles to successfully implement an e-business initiative.

The 4D Framework was applied in the following way:

In the understanding phase, the team did a process redesign that resulted in an organizational change of multiple procurement divisions to one consolidated procurement business process reporting to one vice president of procurement. In the context of e-business, this had to be done rapidly. So, an HVPM process was invoked in the current analysis step to look at the current procurement processes, compare them with available best practices in the industry, and then proceed to an e-procurement process redesign step.

Component-Based Method

Understanding Phase

In this phase, the ABC team did the following:

- They decided on a component-based method.

- They started working on a development and deployment plan. They chose the procurement application to start with. They decided that they had to look across the enterprise to streamline the processes and decided on joint design and ownership.
- The PM created a team with proper roles and responsibilities. It consisted of business analysts, technical architects, programmers, and infrastructure experts.
- Business domain modeling was targeted at IPE. Both the business architecture and technology architecture had that objective so that the components would cater services to ABC and all the partners. These application components formed the basis of a repository.
- They decided on an application development lifecycle methodology/framework. They chose OO methodologies because they knew Unified Modeling Language (UML) and had been using use cases.
- They implemented a transition/change management program to shift from the old habits of application development. They chose more of an architecture/assemble approach rather than code generation. A training program was designed.

Functional requirements

This was one of the first steps taken. ABC's business/systems analysts did the following:

Interviewed users of ABC as well as partners. Based on these interviews, they created a high-level functional requirements document. This document broke down the procurement process into sub-sections and articulated all the requirements in each sub-process. It emphasized the interfaces between the new procurement system and the old legacy systems. There were interface issues with disparate vendor/partner systems (EDI vs. e-commerce vs. paper catalogs vs. simple electronic catalogs, etc.).

Analysis

A high-level analysis was performed with input from the functional requirements gathered.

The team embarked on a technical architecture that included pretty detailed application-level analysis and architecting. Some business object modeling and data modeling were also completed. Use cases were analyzed and expanded.

Using the 4D Framework, the team started thinking about people, process, and within technology, not only the software issues, but the hardware and networking issues also. They did a high-level analysis of the approximate hardware and network requirements for this application. They also started following a vendor selection process to choose different hardware, networking components, and software vendors.

Solutions Phase

Design

With the functional specifications and high-level architecture documents (business, applications, and infrastructure) in place, the ABC team embarked on a detailed architecture and design process. They developed a detailed business object model and mapped application components to it. OO techniques were used to build relationships between objects and encapsulate methods. Technology standards were set, packages were finalized, and a detailed design document with emphasis on components was developed.

The other important aspect was the design/development of the user interface, where the team built a prototype and worked with the users to get the right user experience and a user-friendly application. The right functionalities were also validated and designed.

The design document was updated, fine-tuned, and handed over to the development team. The PM used a project management tool to manage the whole lifecycle of this design/development. The system was now ready for assembly with the application components.

Development

The team used the current Integrated Development Environment (IDE) and component repository to develop the system according to design specifications. Databases were also created according to the database designs developed earlier. Test data was loaded and some unit testing completed.

Implementation Phase

Testing and rollout

The testing group started testing the whole system using a rigorous test plan. They tested each individual module and then also tested the system as a whole. The ABC team ran numerous transactions under different scenarios through the Web so that the system was tested for robustness. Once the testing was completed, ABC was ready to pilot the system with Vendor S, who was most interested in being an electronic partner of ABC.

A cross-enterprise piloting was launched with specific products of Vendor S. ABC could browse Vendor S's Web catalog and order products. The procurement system was based on silent commerce, or Web-enabled EDI, and orders came through the Web to Vendor S correctly. Once the pilot was completed successfully, ABC was ready to launch the application to all other vendors.

▶ Summary

This chapter explained the 4D Framework with its four phases, four e-project management functions, four basic building block elements, and four foundation principles (disciplines). The four dimensions are absolutely critical in the success of any e-business initiative. E-business initiatives are often single-dimensional, with an emphasis either on a new business model or a new technology that skews the whole initiative. This chapter gave a holistic view that all the aspects are needed for the successful implementation of any e-business initiative. Many Net Economy companies need disciplines that have evolved over the years and the 4D Framework serves as the glue for this multidimensional approach. Another interesting point that needs to be noted is that depending on the stage of the e-transition, one or more of the basic building elements may take precedence, but all four of them need to be considered in parallel.

Part 5

Appendices

Assessment

Business Assessment Template
Vision:
Mission:
Markets:
Market Segments:
Market Share:
Growth Rate:

IA= Initial Assessment Phase
U= Understanding Phase
S= Solutions Phase

Financials:

IA: Annual Revenue
IA: Net Income
IA: Growth Rate

U: Inventory Turns
U: Cash Flow
U: Debts
U: Other

Organization:

Division *Heads* *Location* *Budgets*

Reorganization/Reengineering:

U: Known Efforts and Upcoming Changes
S: Additional Details Relevant to Proposed Solutions/Success

Major Projects:

U: Key Project Overviews and Business Goals

Project Name *Organization/Contact* *Description/IT Requirements*

Business Issues:

U: Major Bottlenecks in Business Process

IT Organization Assessment Template
IT Vision:
IT Mission:
Future Plans for People, Process, and Technology:
Formally Articulated IT Principles:
Explicit/Implicit Principles:
Core Architectural Principles (COTS, OO, N-Tier):
Stage for Server Consolidation (1–10):

Financial:

> IA: Annual Budget for IT. Past 3 years, HW/SW purchases, development, and operations
> U: Additional Information—Complete

Let's look at Table A–1.

Table A–1

IT	Year 1	Year 2	Year 3	Industry
Hardware				
Software				
Applications				
Operations				
Mainframe				
Big servers				
Web servers				

Table A–1   (Continued)

IT	Year 1	Year 2	Year 3	Industry
Storage				
Desktops				
Network				
Telecom (voice/data)				
COTS				
Customer development				
Server consolidation				

Was any TCO analysis done in the past?

Interested in a TCO analysis?

Organization:

> IA: Preliminary Survey
> U: Summary of all Relevant Organizational Units

Data Center _Head_ _Location_ _Number of People_ _Budgets_

IT Maturity Level:

What is the management style/sphere of influence in each data center?

How is IT perceived by the users?

Cross-functional teams with users?

Decisions made based on technology merit?

Is enough importance given to partnership, service, and support?

Who does the chief information officer (CIO) report to (e.g., chief financial officer/chief executive officer [CFO/CEO])?

Who are the different vendors and how much business do they do?

Has any data center/application/data consolidation been done?

E-Business Project Management

The four e-business project management functions are:

- **Plan**—The project/program needs to be planned at various levels. A plan with appropriate tasks, completion and start dates, and resource requirements is minimally needed. This plan needs to be revisited and modified frequently, especially in an e-commerce context.

- **Coordinate**—All the parties need to be structured, roles and responsibilities clearly defined, and the PM needs to coordinate all the activities of the e-business project.

- **Control**—The program/project needs to be controlled by checking progress against agreed upon deliverables and milestones. Scope creep is managed and mitigated; risks are constantly reviewed and controlled.

- **Communicate**—A big part of successful e-business project implementation is communication. It is, however, the trickiest and one of the hardest things to do. The cultural differences of the various parties in the team and outside the team can really make it a very complex issue. We believe that there is no such thing as over-communication.

Project Management

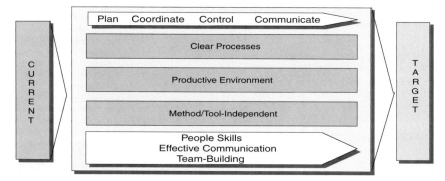

Figure B–1   A comprehensive framework

A comprehensive framework is depicted in Figure B–1.

The weaknesses of current e-business project practices that lead to unsuccessful e-commerce projects are:

- Project scope is not well-defined. This results in mismatched expectations from all sides of the project team, often expanding the scope of the project. Again, even in a well-scoped project, scope changes happen. So, there needs to be a change management process in place. Unfortunately, lots of e-commerce projects, in the rush to produce results quickly, ignore this fundamental rule.

- Project objectives are not in line with the broader organizational goals, resulting in a lack of executive support and the eventual death of the project despite all the other elements being in place.

- The project is managed without any adherence to any framework of processes and methods; it is just an ad-hoc assembly of "stuff" to do "things."

- Project planning and control are inadequate and unbalanced. E-commerce projects need a well-thought-out planning and control mechanism, as opposed to the general myth. They need to be managed against set objectives and corrective actions need to be taken quickly.

- Communication can never be undermined. There are so many components of an e-commerce project and there is so much need for businesspeople and technical people to work together in a tight iterative fashion that effective communication is a critical success factor. There is no such thing as over-communication. The PM needs to emphasize this over and over again, especially in corporate cultures, which do not foster communication.

- The e-business project team structure is not well thought of. Roles and responsibilities are not clearly defined and skill sets do not match positions. A mixture of businesspeople and technical people is not well-orchestrated.

Now these are not just e-business project issues, but general project issues. However, we see these issues becoming absolutely critical to an e-business project's success due to the fact that these projects have shorter release cycles, are rapidly iterative, and are very much driven by customer requirements.

These distinct phases, elements, and disciplines constitute the foundation of the 4D Framework.

▶ The Framework in Detail

The 4D Framework can be used in all kinds of e-initiatives, starting from application development to infrastructure implementation. The 4D Framework can even be used to handle e-engagements (sales or consulting from pre-sales to post-sales and back).

The elements and functions discussed here are not necessarily complete. There can be other elements as required. However, the 4D Framework works in all cases.

In this context, it is appropriate to mention that we have emphasized in this book only those elements that we feel are the most important in understanding and managing e-initiatives. The other related elements have been mentioned, but not emphasized. The elements and methodologies emphasized are project/program management elements, some business analysis techniques, and value chain analysis and value chain linking, which are powerful methodologies for linking e-business drivers with e-initiatives and change management elements. These elements are often neglected and ignored in many e-business projects.

▶ The Phases, Elements, and Functions in Detail

Understanding Phase

The purpose of this phase is to first determine if the e-business project is a go/no go. If it is a go, we must get a detailed understanding of the e-commerce opportunity. This phase will use all the basic building elements and project management functions to create a roadmap of tasks, methodologies, architectures, and project plans.

Some straw-hat elements and project management functions are given in Table B–1. However, the list is limited.

Table B–1 Building Blocks to Task Map

Building Block Elements/Functions	Tasks/Methods/Processes
Business Elements	Business case analysis Business modeling Business-to-technology linking methods Business process maps (high-level) Business architectures (high-level)
People Elements	Cultural analysis Team cultural analysis Training/mentoring Skills analysis Job descriptions
Process Elements	Process (any) modeling Rapid, iterative methods Policies, procedures, etc. IPE Change management Software change management Request for Information/Quote(RFI/RFQ) process (for pre-sales e-commerce engagements)
Technology Elements	Process modeling Data modeling DFDs Technology architectures Use cases Package evaluation Service level agreements—QoS (high-level)

Building Block Elements/Functions	Tasks/Methods/Processes
PM Functions	E-project plan
	Kickoff meeting
	Roles and responsibilities
	E-business project status
	Communication plan

Solutions Phase

The purpose of this phase is to provide a solution (or solutions) for the e-commerce initiative. Some solutions can address the following:

1. Build (using, say, component-based methodologies)

2. Buy (and integrate)

3. E-commerce infrastructure solutions (intranets, the Internet, etc.)

4. Rent (using application service providers [ASPs])

The 4D Framework is flexible and can incorporate any solution as demanded by the customer's needs. The solutions phase is not just giving a technology solution, it deals with business, relationships, and other relevant issues and gives an integrated solution.

Table B–2 gives a sample of tasks related to the different functions in the Solutions phase.

Table B–2   Building Blocks to Task Map

Building Block Elements/Functions	Tasks/Methods/Processes
Business Elements	Business modeling (detailed)
	Gap analysis
	Business-to-technology linking methods
	Business process maps (detailed level)
	Business architectures (detailed level)
	Objectives and metrics
	Content inventory

Table B–2 Building Blocks to Task Map (Continued)

Building Block Elements/Functions	Tasks/Methods/Processes
People Elements	Culture analysis Team culture analysis Training/mentoring Skills analysis Job descriptions
Process Elements	Process (any) modeling Rapid, iterative methods Policies, procedures, etc. Change management Software change management Quality assurance process Site support process
Technology Elements	Process modeling (detailed) Data modeling (detailed) DFDs Technology architectures Design specifications Workflows Systems integration Use cases IPE Interface design Information engineering Package evaluation Service level agreements—QoS
PM Functions	E-project plan (detail) Kick-off meeting Regular status meetings Roles and responsibilities E-project status Communication plan (detail) Deployment plan

Implementation Phase

This phase again has all the elements needed to do a successful implementation. The team will select from the repository of tasks, methods, and processes of the framework to create its implementation plan. Different types of solutions will have different implementation plans. Please see Table B–3 for a comprehensive set of tasks at this phase.

Table B–3   Building Blocks to Task Map

Building Block Elements/Functions	Tasks/Methods/Processes
Business Elements	ROI metrics for implementation Revisit use cases
People Elements	Cultural analysis Team cultural analysis Training/mentoring Skills analysis Job descriptions
Process Elements	Process (any) modeling Rapid, iterative methods Policies, procedures, etc. IPE Software change management Maintenance matrix
Technology Elements	Technology architectures Hardware/software integration Performance requirements Software/hardware rollout Use cases Package implementation Service level agreements – QoS (detailed)
PM Functions	Implementation plan Kickoff meeting Status meeting Roles and responsibilities E-business project status Communication plan Maintenance plan (high-level)

Case Study

As a multinational company, YXZ manufactures automobiles sold around the world under different brand names. The company competes in the truck parts aftermarket, primarily through its dealer network. Additionally, YXZ also sells general automotive parts and accessories through retail outlets.

YXZ products are sold in a number of countries. Some of these countries include the United States (U.S.), Canada, Australia and the United Kingdom (U.K).

YXZ maintains exceptionally high standards of quality for all its products: they are well-engineered, highly customized for particular applications, and sell in the premium segment of their markets, where they have a reputation for superior performance and pride of ownership.

YXZ is a decentralized company with each of the operating divisions having its own policies and procedures for procurement, billing, HR, and payroll. The result of this decentralization is that a very varied set of applications are installed across the company.

YXZ has embarked on a project to upgrade or replace its HR and payroll systems with a Web-enabled HR system. The organization undertook such a project due the following limitations and drawbacks of the current systems:

- The existing HR software is inadequate given the increase of staff in the past five years
- Unacceptable user dial-in access to the local area network-based HR software bundle
- Duplicate data entry and redundant business processes
- Unacceptable access speed and disjointed HR information worldwide

This project identified and selected an off-the-shelf, Web-enabled HR software bundle to serve the needs of the YXZ divisions located within the U.S. based on the HR System Evaluation Team's understanding of the organization's current business processes and needs. The HR System Evaluation Team developed a general system design and documented its desired system functionality in the HR project functional requirements specifications.

The purchase of the off-the-shelf Web bundle was halted at one time because YXZ management felt that the results identified to date were likely insufficient to justify proceeding with a software purchase. These results included:

- A reduction/elimination of clerical data entry staff
- A potential for reduced system support effort
- A potential for improved operations and data integrity
- Ongoing payroll vendor support

▶ 4D Framework and Value Chain Analysis

Before proceeding with the purchase and implementation of a new software application, YXZ used a value chain linking analysis to assess the value of implementing a new HR/payroll solution.

Discussions within YXZ indicated that its HR and payroll systems we closely linked with two other systems: time card and labor (see Figure C–1).

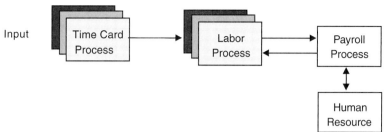

Figure C–1   System relationships

The HR, payroll, labor, and time card systems in use at YXZ today are listed in Table C–1. A variety of different time card and labor systems and processes exist today.

Table C–1   Existing YXZ Systems

Site	Type of System	Name of System
Plant A	Payroll	Mpay
	Labor	Lab
	Human Resource	HRSoft
	Time Card	Excel
Plant B	Payroll	Mpay
	Labor	Lab
	Human Resource	HRSoft
	Time Card	Excel
Plant C	Payroll	Mpay
	Labor	Lab
	Human Resource	HRSoft
	Time Card	Excel
Plant D	Payroll	Mpay
	Labor	Lab
	Human Resource	HRSoft
	Time Card	Excel
XYZ Auto Parts—Retail	Payroll	Mpay
	Labor	Lab
	Human Resource	HRSoft
	Time Card	Point of Sale

These different computer systems do not feed one another, so the users spend a large portion of their time inputting and auditing data.

The HR System Evaluation Team's scope was restricted to the areas of HR, payroll, and labor. Some of the leading labor issues were:

- Scheduling
- Maintenance
- Transaction date
- Payroll cutoff period
- Slow system response time during time approval
- Sign-on requirements
- Visibility of pre-scheduled results
- Labor/staffing approval
- Automatically allocating late or unreported time
- Security over the Web

Objective of the Project

The primary objectives of this effort were:

- To assess the value of and business justification for replacing the existing HR and payroll systems with new solutions based on Web technology
- To investigate and identify additional objectives and results, if any
- To develop and recommend a value chain results map for HR and payroll
- To assist YXZ management and the team with the development and presentation of results to YXZ executives

Project Organization (Program Office)

Using 4D Framework principles, the HR team included membership from various parts of the business. The team members included people from plants, IS, corporate payroll, and corporate (steering committee). It was thus a geographically dispersed, virtual team.

Project Scope

Project scope was originally limited to include HR and payroll. However, the HR team determined that time card and labor should also be included. Failure to include time card and labor in the scope of the project would simply perpetuate the existing silo-like, functional view. The project sponsors agreed to this modification of scope. By using 4D process principles, they knew they had to look at the end-to-end process and not single functional area.

▶ Introduction to the Value Chain Linking Method

The use of the value chain linking method and results chain technique provides a number of HR targeted results. One of the advantages of the method is that it can be used to identify opportunities and specify the appropriate scope and elements involved as well as the associated overall investment bundle. As a method, it can help identify all the different parts of the organization that may be involved. One of the strengths of the method is that it operates regardless of actual organizational structures and of the specific roles and responsibilities of different organizational units. It can be used to support incremental, as well as breakthrough thinking, goals, and objectives while looking at the best ways for an e-investment to profit the organization. Value chain linking was discussed in detail in earlier chapters.

Key Messages from the Value Chain Results

The main value chain results (objectives) of a systems implementation were identified as follows:

1. Increased focus on customer requirements
2. Increased productivity
3. Reduced cost
4. Attracted, hired, and retained highly skilled employees

These four intermediate value chain results affected the final value chain results, which were improved financial results.

Figure C–2 is a high-level value chain link that resulted out of the analysis.

The results chain developed by the HR team also contained three main themes that contributed to the attainment of the stated objectives:

- **People**—The people theme identified results associated with the degree of career management performed by an employee. The baseline situation on the left side of Figure C–2 indicated a change in the employee-employer relationship. Employees are asking for more today than they traditionally have in the past. To attract, hire, and retain highly skilled employees, the team saw a need to share the responsibility for one's career management with the employee. For this to materialize, a number of cultural and policy issues needed to be modified.

- **Process**—Simply changing the way that YXZ does business in the areas of HR, payroll, time card, and labor can contribute to the attainment of the objectives. A change in process would cause the organization to challenge the reasons why its processes flow the way they do. Improvements to process will eliminate steps and redundancies and remove barriers in the organization that prevent it from being more effective.

- **Technology**—The implementation of integrated systems can either automate the work as it is performed today, or it can support the manner of doing work in a new, improved fashion. In either scenario, integrated systems would provide users with more time to perform value-added activities instead of redundant activities.

▶ The Value Chain Results Chain Description

The HR team developed a value chain results map that identified the targeted results desired from the implementation of a new computer system affecting the areas of focus. The high-level value chain results map is shown in Figure C–2.

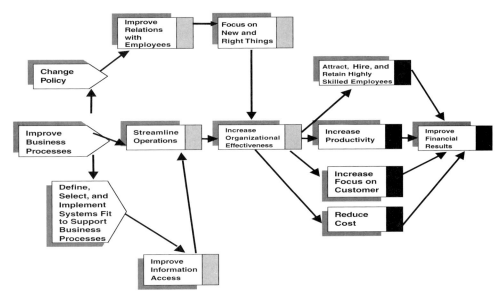

Figure C-2   High-level value chain link

Baseline Results

To do the value chain analysis, the baseline value chain map was constructed. Some of the value chain results are discussed in this section. Next, the team did a targeted value chain results map of the future organization. So it was basically a two-step process. The first step was a to construct a value chain of the current organizational processes and then construct a value chain map for the "future" organizational processes.

> **Extremely slow access to HRSoft**—There are approximately 250 users of HRSoft with 95 PCs in the U.S. and Canada that depend on the information contained within HRSoft to respond to a manager's or employee's request for information. HRSoft is a local network-based product whose network demand exceeds its present capacity. Most users are located remotely and must dial into the HRSoft system to gain access to the information contained within the system.
>
> **Users indicated that they are unable to gain access to HRSoft through the dial-in access**—It would seem that the number of

users has exceeded the present capacity configuration. These delays affect their ability to respond to employee and manager requests and cause frustration. In addition, users have resorted to developing their own standalone systems to maintain the same information that HRSoft carries simply because they are unable to respond effectively with the current status of HRSoft.

Redundancies in HR/time/labor/payroll process, data, applications and business processes exist—The HR, time, labor, and payroll systems are not integrated with one another, and multiple systems and processes even exist within the same functional area. This has resulted in processes that fill in the gaps created by the lack of systems integration. There are several pieces of data that are common to all systems, yet not shared by them. Therefore, each system user has created and supported a set of processes that support the data requirements of its system of choice. In addition, the organizational structure supports process redundancies.

Ownership of information, systems, and processes remains within the boundaries of each system or function—Horizontal, or cross-functional ownership, does not exist today.

Payroll systems vendor can discontinue support of the software—Payroll Vendor P notified YXZ of its intent to discontinue support of its Mpay software bundle. At that time, payroll Vendor P supported 75 clients using Mpay. YXZ implemented Mpay a number of years ago to operate its payroll processes across the entire organization. A short time following Mpay's payroll implementation, YXZ added Mpay's HR features; however, YXZ does not utilize these HR functions today.

In further discussions with payroll Vendor P, the vendor has agreed to continue support of the Mpay product. If, however, payroll Vendor P decides to discontinue its support of the Mpay product, it must notify YXZ one year in advance.

Mpay serves as the vehicle that enables the payroll process to operate on a daily basis. YXZ's version of Mpay has been modified over the years to meet the organization's particular needs. From a functional point of view, users of Mpay indicate that the software's functionality meets their need to pay employees correctly and on time.

If the vendor does not support the product, there are a number of other support options that could be evaluated.

Users can't access information to make timely business decisions— Business users experience difficulty when they need to access information contained within the computer system. In particular, their problems include:

An inability to successfully log on to HRSoft to obtain information via the Web.

Data in the computer is not arranged in a meaningful form and requires that the user manipulate the data to turn it into useful information. This usually means that the user rekeys the data into an Excel spreadsheet to perform additional analysis. The data input must then be checked for data entry errors.

Number of talented job candidates is increasingly difficult to find—YXZ is sensing a high degree of competition for qualified, desirable job candidates. This can decrease the quality of new hires if YXZ does not compete for the best candidates at the same level as other employers. These top candidates are becoming more selective and evaluating a number of different factors as they identify the type of employer they wish to seek. Examples include:

- Cultural environment
- Ability to learn and use new technology
- Access to proper tools to perform work
- Flexibility

Anticipated increase in costs of new hires of good people—The number of employees reaching the age of retirement eligibility is increasing. Replacing these employees will result in an increase in the number of external hires and the associated employment costs.

Targeted Value Chain Results

Some of the value chain results of the future system determined as a result of applying the 4D Framework and value chain analysis were:

Increased focus on customer requirements—Making the customer (internal and external) the focus of motivation will contribute to a win-win situation for the customer and YXZ and translate into doing the "right things" for the "right reasons."

Attracted, hired, and retained highly skilled employees—Retainment of highly skilled employees will help to assure that highly qualified and effective people are available to conduct YXZ's business today and in the future. Retainment of highly skilled employees will result in more internal promotions, higher employee attitude scores, and more efficient training. Silo processes have resulted in redundant activities and multiple ways of doing those activities. This variety in process design has also created a host of challenges in the training area.

Increased productivity—Increased productivity means that resources will be utilized more effectively through:

- More system throughput
- Reduced transaction cycle time
- Less paper
- Less administration costs
- More value-added services
- Fewer information requests as the information is available locally
- Less rework
- Less startup time

Increased financial results—Financial drivers propel YXZ. Achievement of targeted ROI will allow YXZ to continue financial growth and maintain a strong financial position through quality products and services.

Intermediate Value Chain Results

Improved openness—Most information is shared on a need-to-know basis. An open environment is conducive to new ideas, reflects flexibility, and encourages communication.

Increased career management by employee—Transfer the ownership of career management from executives to employees to get the employees more involved in YXZ, keep them interested in staying at YXZ, and support the concept of open communication.

E-initiatives include:

- Establishing employee-managed career development
- Training employees and management
- Changing policy
- Evaluating staff depth
- Establishing employee-based training
- Backfilling employees

Improved YXZ relationship with employees—An overall improvement in the company's relationship with its employees demonstrates that the company values its employees. The employees then focus on the things that will continue to be of value to YXZ and will stay with YXZ.

Improved business climate—Providing employees with the opportunity to make more decisions at the source and to accept responsibility for their own career management will improve the business climate within YXZ.

Decision-making closer to the source—Use the qualified people of YXZ most effectively by allowing them to make decisions. This will improve response time to customers (internal and external) and create a higher sense of value within the employee.

E-initiatives include:

- Redefining decision-making rules
- Redefining roles and responsibilities
- Auditing acceptance
- Changing policy

Increased trust—Giving employees more responsibility will naturally lead to a notion of increased trust between employee and employer.

Improved morale—An improvement to employee morale translates into higher employee satisfaction. Happy, satisfied employees look for new ways to contribute to the organization.

Increased focus on new and right things—Much effort is presently spent on redundant activity. With a shift in the organizational values and implementation of supporting technology, the activities of value are redefined. This redefinition involves a shift in the things that one does, including new things.

Increased organizational effectiveness—Eliminating redundancies in the areas of data entry, process, data, job stream, and reports will enable YXZ to do the following:

- Continue its healthy financial growth and maintain a strong financial position through quality products and services
- Be assured that highly qualified and effective people are available and interested in conducting business at YXZ today and in the future.

Improved enterprise-wide operations—Improving business processes in HR, payroll, time card, and labor will benefit the whole organization.

For example, all employees request information of HR at some point. Improving the process that is used to answer these inquiries affects those in all parts of the enterprise.

Increased revenue—Once the organization is focusing on the right and new things of value, the whole enterprise will experience positive results. All of this can trigger employees to find new ways of generating revenue for YXZ.

Reduced cost—When the organization becomes more effective as a result of its people, process, or technology changes, it can reduce its costs.

Improved information access—With new processes, supporting systems, and tools, users will have more access to the meaningful information required to make business decisions.

E-initiatives include:

- Eliminating duplicate databases
- Eliminating duplicate systems
- Performing data cleanup
- Developing and implementing new procedures
- Setting standards

The effects of the following value chain results will be as follows:

- Improved systems

- Improved business decision flexibility
- Improved responsiveness planning

Increased support systems—Following the improvement of business and technology processes, the information support systems will increase.

E-initiatives include:

- Improving technology processes
- Improving business processes
- Conducting current process assessment
- Identifying, procuring, and implementing technology to support new business requirements

Improved systems—The present-day systems within YXZ are difficult to maintain. An improvement to the business and an implementation of integrated systems will result in a benefit of improved systems that are easier to sustain and maintain.

Increased user-managed system support functions—Users are becoming more sophisticated and wish to accept more responsibility in the area of system support.

E-initiatives include:

- Assessing user skills
- Defining system maintenance requirements
- Setting standards
- Defining new roles and responsibilities
- Training

Improved responsiveness planning—YXZ encourages responsiveness planning to eliminate the element of surprise. Effective systems, tools, and information access will result in improved responsiveness planning.

Improved business decision flexibility—The improvement to information access with a common system and business process approach is designed to offer business decision flexibility to the various business functions.

▶ Value Chain Linking Options

Three main themes and paths emerged from the HR team's development of a value chain link map and 4D Framework elements: people, process, and systems. The value of the targeted results will vary depending on the path that YXZ elects to follow through value chain linking.

The HR team considered these paths along with the options considered by the HR System Evaluation Team to develop a list of results options (see Table C–2). Associated with each option is the team's relative assessment of the option's benefit value to the organization, the degree of change from today's environment, and the amount of change that the organization would experience.

Table C–2 Different Options to Consider

Scale: 1(Low)–10(High)	Expected Return	Degree of Change	Organizational Change
Implement Web interface for HRSoft			
Improve business processes with old systems			
Refocus on labor/time collection and perform no other business process improvements or systems			
Implement integrated HR and payroll system without business process changes			
Improve business processes and implement Web-based systems that accommodate HR, payroll, labor, and time collection			

Recommendation

YXZ's need to change must be driven by some type of business problem. After sorting through the issues, the HR team identified two main problems:

1. Technical limitations prevent users from accessing and using HRSoft.
2. Process and data redundancies are reinforced through separate computer systems and different organizational agendas.

The HR team is sensitive to delivering value to the organization rapidly and effectively. The team recommends that YXZ proceed with a variation of value chain results—namely the first and fourth options (Table C–3 and Figure C–3).

Table C–3   Recommendations

Improve business processes
Focus on HR, payroll, labor, and time card functions
Implement the Web-based HRSoft and payroll
Integrate the HR and payroll systems
Interface labor and time card collection effectively

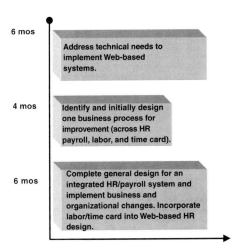

6 mos — Address technical needs to implement Web-based systems.

4 mos — Identify and initially design one business process for improvement (across HR payroll, labor, and time card).

6 mos — Complete general design for an integrated HR/payroll system and implement business and organizational changes. Incorporate labor/time card into Web-based HR design.

Figure C–3   Estimated timeline

Recommended Step and Costs

Steps	Total Cost	Requested Funds
Address the technical requirements.	$250,000	$250,000
Identify and initially design one business process.	$375,000	$375,000
Implement integrated HR/Payroll system and concurrently implement the business and organizational changes.	$575,000	
Interface labor and time card into the HR/Payroll general design.	$ 50,000	$625,000
	Total	$1,250,000

Figure C–4   Costs and results of recommended approach

Costs and Results of the Recommended Approach

The funds requested to implement the recommended steps associated with the suggested approach totals $1,250,000. (See Figure C–4).

The HT team ha identified the present-day operating costs. Each of the targeted value chain results identified by the HR team translates into value for the organization. Some results are more tangible than others; therefore, the HR team has focused on the tangible results to justify the project. The potential improvement ranged from 5–10 times the current costs (See Figure C–5).

System Alternatives

The team considered the different technology alternatives in the value chain results map and did some more analysis. Then they chose the one with the maximum operational flexibility.

Productivity Improvements from Recommended Option		
	Current Cost	Potential Productivity Improvements
	Thousands	**Thousands**
Field Human Resources		
Corporate Human Resources		
Compensation & Benefits		
Corporate Payroll		
Automotive Payroll/HR		
Other Divisions Payroll		
Systems Support/Run Costs		
Administrative Managers Costs		
Total	**$X**	**$ (5X − 10X) RANGE**

Figure C–5   Productivity improvement cost and results

▶ E-Business Project Management Functions (Tasks)

These tasks are used to do project management at different phases. Project management tasks can be used in any context with any other task. Distinct categories of tasks can be grouped together. However, as has already been articulated, the 4D Framework has kept rigid dependencies and categorizations as minimal as possible.

Project management tasks can be divided into four logical functions: plan, coordinate (and structure), control, and communicate.

Plan

This set of tasks is normally conducted at the beginning of an e-business project. The tasks are:

- Define scope of project to clearly establish the boundaries of the project. Define what will be included and what will not be included.

- Define roles and responsibilities to establish who will do what and their interactions.
- Define communication plan to establish the mode, frequency, and structure of communication within the core team and outside. Status meetings, email, and weekly updates are all preplanned and discussed within the team.
- Create plans and procedures to establish project plans, resources, dates, and team policies/procedures in whatever depths agreed to by the team.
- Create statement of work tasks and produce a document that highlights the project in its entirety, so that all parties agree and sign off.
- Do cost analysis to establish a cost basis for the project, for tracking purposes and handling the expectations of the client.
- Establish a formal procedure for project approval and sign-off.

Coordinate

After the initial planning phase, the project is actually activated and team equipped. The primary task is to communicate the plan to the team. The project plan, milestones, roles, responsibilities, and other project-related information are communicated to the team. This ensures that the team understands the project goals and knows who is responsible for what tasks and deliverables

Control

The project manager keeps control of the project by communicating and checking actual tasks completed against planned milestones. The project manager adjusts resources and schedules to costs, according to necessity

Communicate

The project manager's core job is to communicate clearly and effectively with his or her team, the steering committee, and other organizations affected by the customer. The project manager does this via written, verbal, and electronic means.

Example of Change Control Templates

The following templates can be used very effectively in creating a change management program for an e-business transformation. These templates can be used in a multi-step process of change management and communication.

All the change initiatives can be gathered and controlled via a master change control map, which helps to summarize the communication for key stakeholders in the program and the status. (See Figure D–1.)

▶ Master Change Control Plan

A benefit of this plan is that it gives a status summary of who is targeted and the results (Figure D–2). It should ask the following questions:

1. Any ideas/tasks need validation?
2. Any further actions need follow-up?
3. Timeline?

Communication Plan

Where?	Who?	How?	Why?
Newsletters	Employees	Newsletter	• Effect change • Reinforce benefits • Results
Letter from Senior Executive	Employees	Targeted Letter	• Vision of new process • Show change • Future roadmap
Face-to-Face	Employees	Useful Information	• Reinforce ideas/plans/benefits • Team • Feedback
Town Hall Meetings	Employees	In-Person	• Inspire/motivate • Share success • Future roadmap

Figure D–1   Communication plan sample

This map is linked to a communication template (see Figure D–3), which helps to plan meetings/events/communications, create targeted messages, capture feedback, and bring up issues.

The detailed follow-up template allows detailed planning targeted for key stakeholders/divisions (see Figure D–4). There will be one such template per stakeholder or targeted organization, whatever the case may be. This allows the communications issues to be kept right on target with due accountability and carry the momentum of the change management process.

An overall communication plan will be a process that allows the tracking of communications and stakeholder concerns, including:

Master Change Control Plan

Title & Name	Dept.	Date	Discussion/ Presentation	Results	Follow-up Action	Needs	Impact

Figure D–2   Master change control plan

1. Master change control plan to keep track of the progress of executive/stakeholder communications.
2. Individual communication plan, which plans for individual meetings and also validates against the master change control plan.
3. Follow-up plan, which plans for follow-up activities and keeps alignment with the overall change process.

How We Benefit from Each Step of the Communication Process
Individual Communication Plan

Name of Interviewer:
Name of Interviewee:
Date:

Planning Horizon:

Feedback:

Purpose:

Focused Messages:

Issues, Concerns, Questions:

Solution:

Follow-Up Action:

Helps to:

1. Organize individual meetings

2. Create correct messages

3. Plan next steps

4. Map individual messages to group dynamics

5. Request continuous feedback

Figure D–3   Individual Communication Plan

How We Benefit from a Communication Process
Follow-Up Plan

Name:
Date:
Context of Communication:
Planned Next Steps:
What?
How?
When?
Who?
Why?

Benefits:
- Continuous communication

- Link between top-level communication and individual or group

- Tighten up loose issues

- Strategic alliance

Figure D–4   Follow-up plan

Index

Page numbers ending in "f" refer to figures.
Page numbers ending in "t" refer to tables.

Mobile team, 126
Models, 153–54
Monitoring phase. *See* Maintenance/monitoring phase
Morale, 261
MPay software, 258
Multidimensional information, 26
Multidimensional outlook, 64, 65f, 89
Multidirectional communication, 26

N

"Nature of change" identification, 161–77
Needs-based power, 175
.NET, 21
Net Economy, 13–14, 14f, 16–17, 33, 66
Netmosphere, Inc., 203
Netscape, 196
Network architecture, 211, 212f
Networking, 24, 175
New Economy, 66, 68
Non-traditional competition, 22–23

O

Object-oriented programming, 212–14
Old Economy, 15, 23, 24, 68
Online auctions, 25, 45
Open environment, 260
Opportunity recognition, 94–96
Oracle, 48, 197, 198, 216
Organization, 167f, 168–69
Organizational components, 192, 193t
Organizational culture
  change process, 74t–75t
  entrepreneurship, 172
  explanation of, 160
  external focus, 171
  flexibility, 171
  hierarchy culture, 172–73
  internal focus, 171
  issues, 171–73
  model of, 154, 166–71, 167f, 173–77, 174f, 205
  rational management, 172

team culture, 171
understanding, 72–73
Organizational decision-making, 161, 161t
Organizational effectiveness, 262
Organizational learning, 72
Organizational modeling, 205
Organizational power model, 154, 173–77, 174f
Organizational process model, 154, 166–71, 167f
Organizational transformation initiatives, 145–47
Organizational units, 175, 176f
Organizations
  alignment actions, 150, 151
  business elements, 203–6
  change management, 149–51
  dimensions of, 157–60, 157f
  direct actions, 150, 151
  mitigations, 150, 151
  people elements, 206–10
  technology elements, 210–19
  transitions, 150, 151
  understanding, 149

P

Pacific Edge Software, Inc., 203
PCs, 59
People analysis, 210
People drivers
  components of, 193t
  customer value, 14
  e-business and, 26–29, 184–85, 184f
  e-initiatives and, 188t
  explanation of, 9
  objectives, 256
  role of, 37
People elements, 153, 206–10, 246t
Peoplesoft, 216
Performance evaluations, 209
Performance management, 229
Performance matrix, 131, 132f